TO:

....

FROM:

....

DATE:

....

Praise for *The Secret Garden Devotional*

"With the skill of a master gardener and the gentle hand of a friend, Rachel guides us through Mary's path and garden to show us the seeds of wisdom and wonder that have been planted there all along. She then sows these truths deep into our hearts with a special blend of biblical knowledge, purposeful prayer, and real-life application."

— **KERI WILT**, motivational speaker, writer, and Heart Cultivator at www.TheWell-TendedLife.com and the great-great-granddaughter of Frances Hodgson Burnett, author of classics like *The Secret Garden*

"Each year we hold on to the hope that the sun will shine after the darkness of winter, in order for new life to burst forth from the gardens we cultivate. Rachel Dodge has given us such an eloquent reminder in *The Secret Garden Devotional* that no matter how bleak our surroundings might look, new life is stirring just below the surface to be revealed at the most opportune time—God's perfect time! We can each do ourselves a favor by spending some intentional moments with this book to cultivate the garden in our hearts."

— **JEN SMITH**, book collector, photographer, and curator of Storybook Style (@storybookstyle)

"This devotional beautifully teases out the story of God's love, faithfulness, and redemption quietly woven throughout the pages of a beloved classic. You'll find encouragement and personal insight as you reread Mary Mary Quite Contrary's story, this time through the lens of God's redemptive love."

— **JULIE FISK**, co-author of five devotionals, including *The One Year Daily Acts of Friendship Devotional* and *One Good Word A Day: 365 Invitations to Encourage, Deepen, and Refine Your Faith*

"*The Secret Garden Devotional* pulls themes from the novel that touch our hearts and nurture our souls, so we can relish the garden as a place of hope, recognize seasons of change, and above all, remember that spring will come again soon. It reminds us that there's a bigger picture and offers hope that we will grow and blossom again in time. Rachel's choice of encouraging verses for each devotional entry, alongside the prayers she wrote, remind us that we're never alone, God is for us, God protects and shelters us, and God sings over us. The illustrations are enchanting as well."

— DEB GRUELLE, bestselling author of *Ten Little Night Stars* (Zonderkidz) and *Aching for a Child* (David C. Cook)

"In sixth grade, I got a toy padlock and key from the prize box at the dentist's office and pretended it was my key to the secret garden. That's how in love I was with the story. But it wasn't until adulthood that I truly appreciated the beauty of *The Secret Garden*. Rachel Dodge's devotional takes that beauty to an even deeper level by uncovering what it can teach us about hope, renewal, friendship, and our ultimate healing through Christ. Thank you, Rachel, for bringing this favorite classic to life in a new way."

— JEANETTE HANSCOME, multi-published author and speaker

"*The Secret Garden* was the first book I ever fell in love with, and it has become my children's favorite read-aloud. Having read it nearly every year since I turned ten, Mary, Dickon, Colin, Ben, and Martha have become cherished friends, and they often call me to lose myself in a world where blossoms and children are hidden behind locked doors. Rachel's devotional is the perfect companion to this beloved classic. She gently pulls lessons from each chapter and grows them with the tenderness of a gardener. *The Secret Garden Devotional* is meant to be read aloud, children delighting over the charming illustrations and teenagers discovering connections between a beloved story and spiritual truths."

— KIMBERLY DUFFY, author of *Every Word Unsaid* and *The Weight of Air* (February 2023)

The
SECRET
GARDEN
Devotional

A Chapter-by-Chapter Companion
to the Beloved Classic

Rachel Dodge

BARBOUR
PUBLISHING

Cover and interior illustrations by Anastasia Nesterova.

Published by Barbour Publishing, Inc., 1810 Barbour Drive, Uhrichsville, Ohio 44683, www.barbourbooks.com

Our mission is to inspire the world with the life-changing message of the Bible.

ecpa Member of the Evangelical Christian Publishers Association

Printed in China.

*To my dear family for their love and support.
And for my grandmother Delores Beckman who
gave me my first copy of* The Secret Garden
and inspired me to become an author like her.

*"It was the sweetest, most mysterious-
looking place anyone could imagine."*

FRANCES HODGSON BURNETT,
The Secret Garden

CONTENTS

A
SECRET GARDEN
WELCOME

"The LORD will guide you continually, giving
you water when you are dry and restoring
your strength. You will be like a well-watered
garden, like an ever-flowing spring."

ISAIAH 58:11 NLT

My grandmother mailed a beautifully illustrated edition of *The Secret Garden* by Frances Hodgson Burnett to me when I was in the fourth grade. Inside, she wrote these words: *Welcome to the sweetest, most mysterious-looking place anyone could imagine.* As I read the first few pages, I fell in love immediately.

That was the first day of a lifetime of wonderful memories "in the garden" and through the long corridors and winding passages of Misselthwaite Manor. *The Secret Garden* is a novel I read on repeat as I was growing up, and I still keep coming back to it as an adult. I love to lose myself in the magic and mystery of that hidden garden, a place where I can slip away, quiet my heart, and find peace. It reminds me that healing, restoration, and new life are always possible—no matter how trying the circumstances or how difficult the situation.

In a profusion of aching sweetness, *The Secret Garden* also bursts with themes and motifs that can teach us deep spiritual truths when we look at them through the lens of faith. Like the garden itself, our hearts must be carefully tended and cultivated. When we neglect the care and keeping of our souls, metaphorical weeds choke out new growth and thorny branches go unpruned. Seeds of bitterness take root, the soil of our hearts becomes hard, and life falls into a state of disrepair. In contrast, our lives bloom when we consistently sow to the spirit.

If we think of God as a wise and gentle gardener, we see how He faithfully tends to our hearts and carefully pulls up weeds, trims away tangles, and prunes back dry branches. As we invite Him into our everyday moments, He clears space for tender shoots of hope and joy to take root. He waters and fertilizes the places that are wilting and undernourished. He revives and replenishes our dry spots and causes them to flourish and bear fruit.

The Secret Garden also offers meaningful symbols we can examine from a biblical perspective. There is a "robin who showed the way," a door that leads into the garden, and a key that unlocks the door. Mary Lennox's continual search for the way into the garden reminds us to seek after God with all our heart. The buried key and the hidden door to the garden are reminiscent of the steps of faith we take on the road to knowing Christ—the way, the truth, the life

(John 14:6). There is one door that leads to the remission of sins and eternal life with God. The key to that door is faith in Jesus Christ.

Mary's fictional story also provides rare insights into God's faithfulness in every season. There is an ebb and flow in the different stages of life and a season for everything under the sun (Ecclesiastes 3:1). There are summer seasons of harvest and bounty, autumn months of pruning and planning, and winter seasons of digging and waiting.

Best of all, *The Secret Garden* reminds us that spring *is* coming! No matter how dry or barren things might look, our lives can and will blossom again under the gentle care of our Lord. He can bring order out of chaos, restore that which was lost, and cause His people to flourish—even after a long winter season. He plants seeds of revival, bringing to life things that look dead. By His power, our lives and relationships can burst into full and glorious bloom once more because Jesus is in the business of making all things new (Revelation 21:5)!

———————— ◆◈◆ ————————

Are you in need of personal revival? Have you experienced a long winter season or an extended drought? *The Secret Garden Devotional* is designed to fill you to overflowing with the faith, hope, and courage you need to thrive in your daily walk with Jesus. God is ready and waiting to meet with you and encourage your heart as you sit down with Him each day to read, pray, and soak up His Word.

Inside this book, you'll find inspiration and practical tools for tending the garden of your heart. This book contains one devotional entry for every corresponding chapter of *The Secret Garden*, plus three bonus chapters, giving you a 30-day journey with Jesus. Each entry includes quotes, themes, and lessons from that chapter of the novel, thoughts for personal reflection, key Bible verses and scripture application, and a short prayer.

When you sit down to read, have your Bible, a notebook, and a pen handy. You may want to keep your favorite copy of *The Secret Garden* close by as well. Open your time with prayer and ask Jesus to speak to your heart in a personal way. Ask Him to restore your soul and spark a renewed passion for His Word. Invite Him to water the dry places of your heart, plant new seeds of faith, and usher in a fresh wind of revival.

Are you longing to blossom and bloom in your faith? If you're ready to experience a season of renewal and a deeper walk with Jesus, the journey begins now!

DAY 1
Never Alone

"The LORD himself goes before you and will be with you; he will never leave you nor forsake you. Do not be afraid; do not be discouraged."

DEUTERONOMY 31:8 NIV

*"Why was I forgotten?" Mary said,
stamping her foot. "Why does nobody come?"*
(CHAPTER 1)

In the opening scenes of *The Secret Garden*, cholera "in its most fatal form" sweeps through Mary Lennox's home in India. Her parents—who are much too interested in parties, finery, and their own selfish lives to ever have spent much time with Mary—both die in the outbreak. Even the servants, who were Mary's caretakers, all die or run away in fear. In the "confusion and bewilderment" of the outbreak, Mary hides away in the nursery and is "forgotten" by everyone: "Nobody thought of her, nobody wanted her. . ."

When Mary wakes up to silence on the third day, the house is "perfectly still" with "neither voices nor footsteps." Two British officers come through the deserted bungalow and find Mary standing in the nursery all alone. Shocked at her presence, having assumed "the child no one ever saw" had died, one officer says, "She has actually been forgotten!" Mary stamps her foot and asks, "Why does nobody come?" The other officer blinks, as if to "wink tears away," and explains to Mary the sad truth: "There is nobody left to come."

It's in this "strange and sudden way" that Mary finds out she has "neither father nor mother left." She's never really known her parents, but now she finds herself utterly alone. It's as though the ground has shifted under Mary's feet; nothing is as it should be. And though Mary will later be transplanted to a new home where she will grow and flourish, put down deep roots, and be made whole again, all she can see in this moment is what she's lost.

In the midst of painful trials, it's hard to see what possible good God could bring from it. We often feel like Mary Lennox—bewildered and alone. But take heart: Your heavenly Father knows the plans He has for you, "plans to prosper you and not to harm you, plans to give you hope and a future" (Jeremiah 29:11 NIV). He is able, "through his mighty power at work within us, to accomplish infinitely more than we might ask or think" (Ephesians 3:20 NLT). He can bring beauty from the ashes of our deepest losses (Isaiah 61:3).

In the Bible, Ruth's story of love and redemption was actually set in motion by tragedy. When her husband died, life as she knew it in Moab ceased. And though she could have stayed in Moab with her family where it was familiar and safe, Ruth bravely chose to go with Naomi to Judah and follow the one true God (Ruth 1). Ruth trusted God with her future, and God protected her and provided for her (Ruth 4). He blessed her with a new husband and a child—and even gave her an honored place in the genealogy of Jesus (Matthew 1:5)!

He alone is my rock and my salvation,
my refuge; I will not be shaken.

PSALM 62:6 NASB

―――――――◦◦◦―――――――

PERSONAL APPLICATION:

Are you facing a painful ending? Do you feel uprooted or alone? Be assured of this: God has not forgotten or abandoned you. "I will not forget you! See, I have engraved you on the palms of my hands" (Isaiah 49:15–16 NIV). He goes before you, He is with you, and He will *never* leave you or forsake you (Deuteronomy 31:8). You are His forever.

Life is full of changes and uncertainties, trials and turmoil, but you can be firmly rooted and grounded in the love of Christ (Ephesians 3:17). God's "unfailing love for you will not be shaken" (Isaiah 54:10 NIV). His faithful love endures *forever* (Psalm 136:1). Take this time now to pray and ask Jesus to be your rock and your firm foundation. Trust in Him "with all your heart and lean not on your own understanding; in all your ways submit to him, and he will make your paths straight" (Proverbs 3:5–6 NIV).

PRAYER FOR TODAY:

Dearest Jesus, thank You for loving me and for taking care of me. Thank You for reminding me that my story is not finished and that You have good plans for me. Help me stand firm in my faith and remain rooted and grounded in Your love in the midst of my circumstances. In the areas where I feel alone, I ask for Your comfort and encouragement. Please reveal Your plans and purposes for my life and give me a glimpse of the bigger picture You have in mind for this area of my life: [your prayer]. In Jesus' name, amen.

"Though the mountains be shaken and the hills be removed, yet my unfailing love for you will not be shaken nor my covenant of peace be removed," says the LORD, who has compassion on you.

ISAIAH 54:10 NIV

DAY 2
Shelter in the Storm

You are my hiding place;
you will protect me from
trouble and surround me with
songs of deliverance.

PSALM 32:7 NIV

Other children seemed to belong to their fathers and mothers, but [Mary] had never seemed to really be anyone's little girl.

(CHAPTER 2)

Mistress Mary Quite Contrary can't make her garden in India grow because it's made of wilted flowers that have been plucked from their stems and stuck into the ground. In this chapter, Mary feels just as lifeless and uprooted. She's lost her parents, her home, and her bearings—all within a few days. All she can do is wait unhappily as the arrangements for her future are made by people she doesn't know. And when her fate is decided, she finds out she's being sent across the sea to live in a "great, big, desolate old house" in England with an uncle she's never met.

At the clergyman's home where she's staying, Mary is so "disagreeable" that "nobody [will] play with her" and the children call her Mistress Mary Quite Contrary. But living in "other people's houses" and traveling with other people's families causes Mary to think "queer thoughts" which are "new to her." She notices that she "never seemed to belong to anyone even when her father and mother had been alive." While other children seem to "belong" to their parents, Mary realizes she's "never seemed to really be anyone's little girl."

Mary has always had everything she wants, but she has never had what she truly needs: love and affection. She's had "servants, and food and clothes," but no one has ever "taken any notice of her." Even her mother "scarcely ever looked at her." When cholera broke out, her parents didn't run to protect her; instead, she was completely overlooked. And now, when she needs protection and understanding, she finds herself at the mercy of total strangers.

When it feels like life is happening *to* you, be assured that God is in control. When things change in ways you wouldn't choose, when it seems like you've been overlooked, remember that "God is our refuge and strength, a very present help in trouble" (Psalm 46:1 NKJV). In every trial, in every problem, in every disappointment, God is with you: "Do not fear, for I am with you; do not be dismayed, for I am your God. I will strengthen you and help you; I will uphold you with my righteous right hand" (Isaiah 41:10 NIV).

When Paul was shipwrecked in Acts 27, he was traveling as a prisoner with absolutely no say in where he was going or how he would get there. He experienced a hurricane-force storm, went without food or water for two weeks, and finally had to swim to safety—all because other people didn't heed his warning to wait (Acts 27:10–11). But through it all, Paul believed his life was in God's hands. He chose to pray and break bread and praise God *in* the storm

(Acts 27:35–36). He trusted God and instructed everyone on board to do the same and told them what they needed to do to stay alive. No matter where he went, Paul knew he belonged to God.

> *"Call upon Me on the day of*
> *trouble; I will rescue you."*
>
> PSALM 50:15 NASB

------◆◆◆------

PERSONAL APPLICATION:

When the storms of life rage and you feel forgotten or overlooked, remember that you are not alone—you belong to God! As a follower of Jesus, you are a child of God (John 1:12), an adopted son or daughter (Ephesians 1:5), and a coheir with Christ (Romans 8:17). Nothing can ever separate you from the love of God (Romans 8:38–39).

And notice this: even though Mary felt completely alone in this chapter, there were, in reality, people to watch over her and help her every step of her journey. In your life, God's provision might not look the way you want it to look, but He's providing for you just the same. He is your shelter in the storm (Isaiah 25:4) and your hiding place (Psalm 32:7). In your time of need, His care and His people are all around you—like a safety net.

PRAYER FOR TODAY:

Thank You, Father, for always watching over me. Thank You that I belong to You as Your beloved child. When life gets chaotic and spins out of control, please hold me close in the shadow of Your wings. Calm the storm within me and around me. As I meditate on the verses in this chapter, please help me take them to heart for myself and share them with someone else this week. In the areas of my life where I feel most vulnerable, please be my anchor: [your prayer]. In Jesus' name, amen.

"Indeed, the very hairs of your head are all numbered. Don't be afraid; you are worth more than many sparrows."

LUKE 12:7 NIV

(DAY 3
Unfamiliar Territory

*By faith Abraham obeyed when he
was called to go out to the place
which he would receive as an
inheritance. And he went out, not
knowing where he was going.*

HEBREWS 11:8 NKJV

Mary felt as if the drive would never come to an end and that the wide, bleak moor was a wide expanse of black ocean through which she was passing on a strip of dry land.
(CHAPTER 3)

Mary sees Missel Moor for the first time on a dark, rainy night as she travels by carriage to Misselthwaite Manor, "a house with a hundred rooms nearly all shut up—a house standing on the edge of a moor." Her first glimpse reveals "nothing" but "dense darkness" on either side of the carriage, a "rough-looking road" passing through "bushes and low-growing things," and a "great expanse of dark. . . spread out before and around them."

Mrs. Medlock describes the moor as "miles and miles and miles of wild land that nothing grows on but heather and gorse and broom, and nothing lives on but wild ponies and sheep." Mary thinks the "wide, bleak moor" is like a "wide expanse of black ocean," with the road cut through it like a "strip of dry land." Even the wind makes a "singular, wild, low, rushing sound." She pinches her thin lips together, saying, "I don't like it. . .I don't like it."

At the house, there are no friendly lights or open doors to welcome Mary to her new home. The house is dark, and the "massive" front door is studded with "big iron nails" and crossed with "great iron bars." Mary stands in the "enormous" great hall, feeling "small and lost and odd," amid "dimly" lit portraits and suits of armor. A lone servant says Mr. Craven doesn't want to see her, and Mary is taken "unceremoniously" to her room and left alone. The chapter ends with this: "It was in this way Mistress Mary arrived at Misselthwaite Manor and she had perhaps never felt quite so contrary in all her life."

The road to Misselthwaite isn't pretty, and the welcome isn't friendly—but that doesn't mean there aren't wonderful things in store for Mary in that strange, wild place. And the same is true for you. When you find yourself walking in wilderness places, when the road is rough and narrow, when the destination isn't what you expected, that doesn't mean God can't do something beautiful in that place. Some beginnings are underwhelming; some first impressions aren't great. But keep this in mind: some of God's greatest gifts come wrapped in plain packages.

Mary's drive through the moor "on a strip of dry land" is reminiscent of the Israelites crossing the Red Sea "on dry ground, with a wall of water on their right and on their left" (Exodus 14:22 NIV). The road out of Egypt wasn't easy, and the wilderness beyond the Red Sea was foreign and unforgiving. But every step of the way, God directed the Israelites' steps—with a cloud by day and a pillar of fire at night (Exodus 13:21). He provided them with resting places, manna to eat, and water to drink. Their clothes and sandals did not wear out (Deuteronomy 29:5). Even though they walked in the wilderness, they had everything they needed.

> *"See, I am sending an angel ahead of you*
> *to guard you along the way and to bring*
> *you to the place I have prepared."*
>
> EXODUS 23:20 NIV

PERSONAL APPLICATION:

Mary's first impression of Missel Moor isn't positive, but there's a secret Mary has yet to learn: the wild places of the moor will bloom and burst forth with life at just the right time. In the same way, there are wilderness places in your life and heart where God is preparing the ground for a new work. Though you cannot see it now, there will be a day when even the most rough and tangled parts of your life will bloom again.

Do you feel "small and lost and odd" in your current circumstances? If you find yourself in unfamiliar territory or you don't know the way forward, remember that God not only sees the road ahead clearly—He also designed the map! He is right beside you every step of the way, marking out the path before you. "He will not let your foot slip—he who watches over you will not slumber" (Psalm 121:3 NIV). He will "provide a broad path for [your] feet, so that [your] ankles do not give way" (Psalm 18:36 NIV).

PRAYER FOR TODAY:

Lord, thank You for walking with me on this road. When I feel unsettled and in limbo, please steady me. When I don't know the way ahead, please light up my next steps. When the way is narrow, widen the path and give me a spacious place for my feet to tread. I want to fix my eyes on You, Jesus my Savior. Hem me in behind and before and help me trust You in the unknowns. You are my constant, my everything, my home. I ask You now to speak into this wilderness area of my life: [your prayer]. In Jesus' name, amen.

Your word is a lamp to guide my feet and a light for my path.

PSALM 119:105 NLT

DAY 4
Handpicked Companions

*Walk with the wise
and become wise.*

PROVERBS 13:20 NIV

[Mary] began to feel a slight interest in Dickon, and as she had never before been interested in anyone but herself, it was the dawning of a healthy sentiment.
(CHAPTER 4)

Mary meets three new characters in this chapter—people who challenge her and help her grow. And though she might not have chosen any of them as her companions, each one is just what she needs to flourish and bloom. First, there's the delightful Martha, a Yorkshire servant girl who isn't intimidated by Mary. When Mary calls her a "strange servant," Martha laughs "without seeming the least out of temper" and agrees. Martha challenges Mary's attitudes on servants, poverty, and her own spoiled, haughty ways and gives Mary curious new things to think about.

Then there's Ben Weatherstaff, the cranky old Misselthwaite gardener who is just as contrary as she is. Ben points out their similarities, saying, "We're neither of us good lookin' an' we're both of us as sour as we look. We've got the same nasty tempers, both of us, I'll warrant." His "plain speaking" is a new experience for Mary, who has "never heard the truth about herself in her life." She feels "uncomfortable" at first, but it helps her recognize her own surly ways.

Finally, Mary meets the robin, who gives Mary a lovely "queer feeling in her heart" because he is so "pretty and cheerful" and seems "so like a person." The robin later becomes an integral part of Mary's journey, but first he helps her see that she's lonely. When she's with the robin, enjoying his companionship, Mary realizes that she often feels "sour and cross" because she's never had a friend! The robin brings out the child in Mary, and she begins to run and hop and play with him up and down the garden walks.

Some seasons of life are lonely—especially after a move, a change, or a loss. And it's particularly difficult to open up your heart and life to new people when you're struggling or overwhelmed. Jesus promises to be that Friend who sticks closer than a brother (Proverbs 18:24) and also provide you with earthly connection and fellowship. You *need* godly people in your life. In fact, God has companions that He has handpicked—*just for you*—for this very season of your life. People to walk alongside you, sharpen you, and encourage you.

When David was on the run from King Saul, a ragtag group of men came to support him: "All those who were in distress or in debt or discontented gathered around him, and he became their commander" (1 Samuel 22:2 NIV). That's not the description one might expect of the people

God would choose to surround and defend His anointed future king! But from that group, God raised up an army of valiant warriors and mighty men (2 Samuel 23). God selected those men for a purpose; they stood by David through thick and thin, bravely fought alongside him in battle, and supported him when he became the new king of Israel.

> *As iron sharpens iron, so one*
> *person sharpens another.*
> PROVERBS 27:17 NIV

PERSONAL APPLICATION:

Do you desire for the Lord to bring mighty men and women of God to walk with you and encourage you? Just as Mary meets many people who add color and depth to her life, God wants to match you up with godly friends. If you're not attending a church or aren't very involved, make it a priority to find a church home and join a small group. Ask God to guide your steps to people who will support you and strengthen you in your faith. God's handpicked companions are the best kind to have.

As God expands our horizons, He also invites us to help expand His kingdom. Notice that Mary had "never before been interested in anyone but herself." Ask the Lord to open your eyes to see the people around you with new eyes, and invite the Holy Spirit to open doors for divine appointments. God can use your personality, friendliness, and love for Jesus to soften the heart of a surly Ben Weatherstaff or a stiff Mary Lennox.

PRAYER FOR TODAY:

Thank You, Lord, for this call to open up the borders of my life and expand my connections. I often stay in my comfort zone rather than branch out to meet new people or try new things. If there is someone I've overlooked or been too busy to notice, please give me new eyes. Make me brave enough to open myself up to new friendships. Please bring godly people into my life who challenge my perceptions of myself and others. I especially pray for a deeper connection with this person: [specific name]. In Jesus' name, amen.

"Enlarge the place of your tent, and let the curtains of your habitations be stretched out; do not hold back; lengthen your cords and strengthen your stakes."

ISAIAH 54:2 ESV

DAY 5
Fighting the Wind

We are hard pressed on every side, but not crushed.

2 CORINTHIANS 4:8 NIV

[Mary] was stirring her slow blood and making herself stronger by fighting with the wind which swept down from the moor.
(CHAPTER 5)

When Mary first comes to Misselthwaite Manor, every day is "exactly like the others." She wakes up, watches Martha build a fire, eats her breakfast, and then gazes "out of the window across to the huge moor." She soon realizes that if she doesn't go outside each day, she will have to "stay in and do nothing." Initially, Mary goes outdoors out of necessity and boredom. She doesn't know that this is "the best thing she could have done."

When Mary goes outside and fights against the wind that sweeps "down from the moor," it makes her stronger. At first, she only runs against the wind to "make herself warm." In fact, she hates the wind because it rushes "at her face" and roars and holds her back "as if it [is] some giant" she cannot see. But going outdoors does something new in Mary physically, emotionally, and mentally. As she walks and runs along the paths, "her slow blood" begins to stir. Fighting the wind strengthens her weak body and lifts her spirits.

Mary's struggle against the cold, relentless wind produces something good. The big breaths of "rough fresh air blown over the heather" fill her lungs with "something" that is "good for her whole thin body," whip "red color into her cheeks," and brighten her "dull eyes." When she sits down to breakfast, she has an appetite and her food "tastes nice." She begins to ask questions, begins to listen, begins to think. She runs and plays and tries to whistle and chirp with the robin, which makes her look "almost pretty." The "fresh wind from the moor" blows the "cobwebs out of her young brain" and begins to "waken her up."

As Christians, we are constantly "fighting with the wind" in the spiritual realm. Standing firm and pushing back against spiritual opposition and warfare, against immorality and wickedness, and against the enemy's darts is exhausting work. It often feels relentless and even futile. But just think what it produces! The Lord is doing a work in you as you swim upstream to follow Him in all your ways and strive to be a light for Jesus. Getting up and going out the door each day—to stand for biblical truth and share the hope of Jesus—is making you stronger.

Paul knew what it meant to fight against the wind. His years of evangelism and church planting were plagued by relentless conflict, physical pain, and extreme exhaustion. Everywhere he went, he faced intense opposition. Nothing he did was easy. But he is the same person who wrote these words: "We also glory in our sufferings, because we know that suffering produces perseverance; perseverance, character; and character, hope" (Romans 5:3–4 NIV). Paul did not shy away from difficulty. He believed that the fight was worth it; he knew that the battle was producing fruit; and he knew that Jesus would win the ultimate victory every time.

I have fought the good fight, I have
finished the race, I have kept the faith.

2 TIMOTHY 4:7 NIV

PERSONAL APPLICATION:

Do you ever feel like you're fighting an uphill battle? Be assured that God will strengthen you for the task at hand. Though you are "hard pressed on every side," Jesus will not allow you to be crushed. Though you may be "perplexed," do not despair. Though you face persecution, He will not abandon you. If you are "struck down," you will not be destroyed. (2 Corinthians 4:8–9 NIV.) He has won the victory and will bring you through.

The best place you can fight a spiritual battle is on your knees. As you come before His throne on your own and with other believers, be assured that God hears your prayers: "It shall come to pass that before they call, I will answer; and while they are still speaking, I will hear" (Isaiah 65:24 NKJV). When it feels like you are under attack, do not be dismayed "for the battle is not yours, but God's" (2 Chronicles 20:15 NKJV).

PRAYER FOR TODAY:

Lord Jesus, thank You that You are beside me in every battle. Please take the opposition I face and use it to make my faith stronger. Holy Spirit, I invite You to blow a fresh wind of revival through my mind, body, and spirit. I am in need of refreshment and renewal. I want to recommit myself to the ministry of prayer and intercession, and I praise You in advance for the victories You will bring. Clothe me in the full armor of God as I step out in faith in this difficult situation: [your prayer]. In Jesus' name, amen.

Be on your guard; stand firm in the faith; be courageous; be strong.

1 CORINTHIANS 16:13 NIV

DAY 6
Wutherin'

God sets the lonely in families.

PSALM 68:6 NIV

*If there was no one else alive in the
hundred rooms there were seven mice
who did not look lonely at all.*

(CHAPTER 6)

In this chapter, as the wind "wuthers" around the house and the rain pours "down in torrents," Mary decides to explore the house. She's intrigued by the idea of one hundred empty rooms, and since she's "never been taught to ask permission to do things," she decides to explore the "huge rambling house" on her own. As she wanders all morning through countless corridors, passageways, and rooms, it's the emptiness of Misselthwaite—of a house that at one time must have been filled with people—that Mary ponders as she goes.

Juxtaposed against the backdrop of the vast, lonely house, there are several warm, "comfortable" scenes that capture Mary's attention. First, there's Martha's description of her family's moorland cottage which holds "fourteen people who [live] in four little rooms and never [have] quite enough to eat"—all of whom seem happy and content, despite being cramped and having so little. Mary enjoys hearing about the children who "tumble about and amuse themselves like a litter of rough, good-natured collie puppies," but she's drawn to Mrs. Sowerby and Dickon most of all. Martha's stories of what "mother" said or did "always [sound] comfortable."

Then there's the bright, lively downstairs world of Misselthwaite, where the servants enjoy a "luxurious life below stairs." There, in the "huge kitchen hung about with shining brass and pewter" and servants' hall, the staff enjoys "four or five abundant meals" a day and a "great deal of lively romping."

Finally, there's a mother mouse with her six baby mice "cuddled up asleep near her" that Mary finds in a "comfortable nest" in the cushion of an old sofa. Though there's "no one else alive in the hundred rooms," the mice don't "look lonely at all."

There is an ache within each of us that longs to be part of a vibrant, loving family. Like Mary, we know it's much more enjoyable to live in a cramped cottage filled with love than to live in a mansion that's empty and lonely. There's a reason we long for friendship and companionship and a warm, cozy nest with the people we love. We aren't designed to live solitary lives. We aren't meant to go "wutherin'" through life, wandering on our own. God created us to live side by side in fellowship—with Him and with other believers.

Before His death, Jesus gave us this promise of a future heavenly home where we will dwell with Him: "In my

Father's house are many mansions: if it were not so, I would have told you. I go to prepare a place for you" (John 14:2 KJV). On that glorious day when we see Jesus face-to-face, we will gather with all the saints and the angels to worship Him forever. There will be "no more death or sorrow or crying or pain" (Revelation 21:4 NLT). Until then, it's our job to help make disciples and invite as many people as we can to join the family of God (Matthew 28:19). There's always room for more in God's house, so let's help fill up the rooms!

> *"Therefore go and make disciples of all nations, baptizing them in the name of the Father and of the Son and of the Holy Spirit."*
> MATTHEW 28:19 NIV

PERSONAL APPLICATION:

The descriptions of Martha's family in the cozy Yorkshire cottage and the boisterous servants in the Misselthwaite kitchen capture Mary's attention immediately. What captivates you in terms of fellowship, church family, and close community? What, if anything, keeps you from joining in? If you are part of a loving community of believers, invite others to join you. You never know who might be walking alone.

If you feel like Mary—like you're sometimes on the

outside looking in—it's okay to let God know that you desire closer fellowship with other believers. Ask Him to expand your vision and open new avenues of community or service within your church and neighborhood. Invite Him to show you what doors to try and which corridors to explore.

PRAYER FOR TODAY:

Dear Jesus, thank You for bringing me into a loving relationship with You. Thank You for taking me out of loneliness and setting me in the family of God. Lead me to places of rich community where I can grow with other believers. Help me bond with my church family and put down roots. In the areas of my life that are settled and comfortable, help me to look outside myself and invite others to join the circle. Please lead me to new opportunities for fellowship and help me overcome these personal hang-ups: [your prayer]. In Jesus' name, amen.

---

*"And if I go and prepare a place for you,
I will come again and will take you to
myself, that where I am you may be also."*
JOHN 14:3 ESV

ᴅAY 7
Springtime Is Comin'

"See, I am doing a new thing! Now it springs up; do you not perceive it? I am making a way in the wilderness and streams in the wasteland."

Isaiah 43:19 NIV

"Th' springtime's on its way. It's a long way off yet, but it's comin'."
(CHAPTER 7)

Mary wakes up one morning after the storm and is astonished to see that the moor has undergone a transformation: the gray mist and clouds have been "swept away in the night," the wind has ceased, and a "brilliant, deep blue sky" arches "high over the moorland." Mary has never "dreamed of a sky so blue" that sparkles "like the waters of some lovely bottomless lake." Even the moor itself is now a soft blue instead of a "gloomy purple-black or awful dreary gray."

Mary, who thought "perhaps it always rained or looked dark in England," is stunned by the dramatic shift. Martha says the "storm's over for a bit" and "th' springtime's on its way." Though it's "a long way off yet," it's surely coming. Mary marvels at the "heavenly color" of the moor and listens in wonder at Martha's description of the gold-colored gorse blossoms, flowering heather, and purple bells. She asks wistfully, "Could I ever get there?" and Martha says she'll ask her mother about having Mary come for a visit at their cottage.

Out in the kitchen gardens, Ben Weatherstaff tells Mary that things are "stirrin' down below in th' dark" under the soil—where she can't see them. Delighted by the idea that hidden things are happening under the soil of the bare-looking flower beds, she runs off to play and run with the robin. When she leans close to talk to him near the long, ivy-covered wall, she glimpses something wonderful in a freshly dug hole that a dog has made in the thawed soil: "An old key which look[s] as if it had been buried a long time." She picks it up and whispers, "Perhaps it is the key to the garden!"

Mary's first glimpses of spring and her discovery of the key to the secret garden carry a timely reminder that God often works in mysterious and hidden ways that are beyond our comprehension. In our winter seasons, when there's no visible or outward sign of change, God is always actively at work. When we don't see any forward progress, His plans and purposes are unfolding and developing in ways we can't imagine. When everything looks bare and wintry, He's working below the surface. And at just the right time, He places the key to His plans and purposes right at our feet. Nothing is impossible with God (Matthew 19:26)!

During the Babylonian captivity, Daniel must have felt as though he would never see or hear any good news of his beloved Jerusalem. The city walls and the temple had been burned beyond recognition, most of the Israelites had been captured or killed, and he himself had lived most of his life in captivity. But Daniel took God at His word that after seventy years, Jerusalem would be rebuilt (Jeremiah 25). Daniel turned to the Lord and pleaded with Him "in prayer and petition, in fasting, and in sackcloth and ashes" (Daniel 9:3 NIV). In response, God sent an angel to speak to Daniel—and soon after, the rebuilding of Jerusalem began.

> *"Since the first day you began to pray for understanding and to humble yourself before your God, your request has been heard in heaven."*
>
> DANIEL 10:12 NLT

PERSONAL APPLICATION:

Are you tired of waiting and praying? Remember that plants don't "grow up in a night"; you have to "wait for 'em." In the same way, there are many situations that require patient waiting. But nothing—not a personal crisis, a difficult relationship, or a deep wound—is too big for God. He can make "a way in the wilderness and streams in the wasteland" (Isaiah 43:19 NIV). Though it may be a "long way off yet," springtime *is* coming.

It's hard to wait when you don't see any movement, but there is much wisdom in waiting for God's plans to unfold. Rushing ahead or making our own plans often causes chaos or confusion. Hold out for God's best, and ask Him to bring to completion the work that He has already begun in you (Philippians 1:6). Remember: God's plans are always more stunning than anything you could come up with on your own.

PRAYER FOR TODAY:

Lord Jesus, I'm thankful that You hold everything in Your capable hands. I trust that You are doing a mighty work in my life, under the surface, even when I can't see it. I will wait for Your plans to unfold so that Your purposes might be accomplished in me. I am praying and waiting for "spring," and I believe You will bring it about at just the right time and in just the right way. In this area of my life, please do a mighty work that only You can do: [your prayer]. In Jesus' name, amen.

And I am sure of this, that he who began a good work in you will bring it to completion at the day of Jesus Christ.

PHILIPPIANS 1:6 ESV

DAY 8
Always Be Ready

*Always be prepared to give
an answer to everyone who
asks you to give the reason
for the hope that you have.*

1 PETER 3:15 NIV

She made up her mind that she would always carry [the key] with her when she went out, so that if she ever should find the hidden door she would be ready.

(Chapter 8)

After Mary finds the key to the secret garden, she dreams of the day when she'll be able to go inside, "shut the door behind her," and "make up some play of her own." But no matter how hard she looks as she walks up and down the walk, she can't find the door. She sees nothing but "thickly growing, glossy, dark green leaves," and she thinks it's rather "silly" to be so near the garden and "not be able to get in." She puts the key in her pocket and decides to keep it with her at all times; that way, if she ever finds the hidden door, she will "be ready."

On the day she finally finds the door, it's "the robin who [shows] the way." She sees him "swaying on a long branch of ivy" outside the secret garden and teases him, saying, "You showed me where the key was yesterday. . . . You ought to show me the door today; but I don't believe you know!" In response, he flies up to the top of the wall and sings "a loud, lovely trill, merely to show off." As Mary steps closer, a "gust of wind" swings aside "some loose ivy trails." She glimpses the "knob of a door" under it and quickly jumps forward to grasp it with her hand.

Overcome with "delight and excitement," her heart begins to "thump" and her hands begin to "shake a little." She pushes the ivy aside and finds something "square and made of iron" with a hole in it. She knows it's the "lock of the door which had been closed ten years" and takes the waiting key from her pocket. Breathing "quite fast with excitement, and wonder, and delight," she opens the door and slips inside. At last, she's "standing *inside* the secret garden."

Just as Mary always keeps the key in her pocket, so we should always be ready to share the love of Jesus with others. As a follower of Christ, you carry the Good News with you everywhere you go! Whether you're on a walk, at the store, or at work or school, you have a precious gift to share with others. With that in mind, keep your eyes open for opportunities each day and ask the Holy Spirit to lead and guide your steps. He will set up divine appointments. He will unlock doors you could never open on your own.

The New Testament story of Philip and the Ethiopian is an incredible example of someone who was ready and willing to share the Good News at any time and in any place. In Acts 8, God sent Philip to talk to an Ethiopian eunuch—a court official of Candace, queen of the Ethiopians—who was seated in a chariot alongside the road, reading the words of the prophet Isaiah. When the man asked Philip to explain its meaning, Philip "opened his mouth, and beginning with this Scripture he told him the good news about Jesus" (Acts 8:35 ESV). The man asked to be baptized, and when they came to some water beside the road, Philip baptized him!

> *"See, I have placed before you an*
> *open door that no one can shut."*
> REVELATION 3:8 NIV

PERSONAL APPLICATION

With all this in mind, there are several lessons we can take with us from this chapter. First, don't bury the key of faith. In other words, don't hide your faith under a bushel. Share Jesus with the people you meet each day. Second, be like "the robin who showed the way." Lead the way and teach others how to know, follow, and love God in practical ways.

Finally, be sure to carry God's Word in your heart (Psalm 119:11). Take time to read and study the Bible for yourself and with others. Be ready to share the Gospel with people and practice sharing your personal testimony with fellow believers. You can also literally carry God's Word with you on small verse cards and give them out to people as the Lord leads. The next time you meet someone who needs an encouraging word, you'll be prepared!

PRAYER FOR TODAY:

Dear Jesus, I am so thankful that You reached out to grab hold of my heart and changed my life. Help me to prepare my heart and mind to share the Good News of Jesus with others. I confess that I sometimes get nervous or forget to look for opportunities, but I want to be ready and willing. Teach me to listen closely to the Holy Spirit and keep my spiritual eyes open. Show me the open doors You have set before me to share the Gospel. Please do a special work to soften the hearts of these people: [specific names]. In Jesus' name, amen.

I have hidden your word in my heart.

PSALM 119:11 NLT

DAY 9
Sow Generously

Whoever sows sparingly will also reap sparingly, and whoever sows generously will also reap generously.

2 CORINTHIANS 9:6 NIV

If it were a quite alive garden, how wonderful it would be, and what thousands of roses would grow on every side!

(CHAPTER 9)

When Mary steps foot inside the secret garden, it is "the sweetest, most mysterious-looking place anyone could imagine." Everywhere she looks—climbing up the high walls, hanging in "long tendrils," spreading over other trees, and making "light swaying curtains"—she sees a gray mist of tangled rosebushes. Mary can't tell if anything is alive anymore, but then she glimpses "sharp little pale green points" poking up out of the soil. She knows that means there is still life in the garden—and she can't wait to get to work and help make it come alive!

Martha and her family see something similar in Mary, a lonely young girl who has a lot of life in her and only needs help and encouragement to blossom into full bloom, and they take an interest in her. When Martha's mother sees a jump rope, she buys it for Mary, even though she has so little and can't afford one for her own daughter. It's a small gesture that comes at a great cost, but Mrs.

Sowerby deems it well worth her "tuppence" because she knows that a jump rope and lots of fresh air and exercise will help Mary grow strong.

When Martha hears that Mary wants a little spade and seed packets for her garden, she shares her own simple writing materials with Mary and dictates a letter to Dickon. She asks him to use the money Mary is sending to buy a small set of gardening tools and packets of seeds and bulbs that are "easy to grow." When Mary asks how she will get them from Dickon, Martha assures her that he will walk over and "bring 'em" to Misselthwaite. Mary is overcome by the generosity of Martha's family members and their willingness to do so much for someone they haven't met.

This chapter paints a picture of how sowing generously—with whatever you have to give—brings joy to the giver and brings about a great harvest. In Mary's life, the generosity of the Sowerby family gives her more than help with her garden; it opens the door to friendship, physical health, a happy heart, and even a growing appetite—both for hearty food and for love and companionship. Though they have little to give, the Sowerbys remind us that when we share what we have with others, God always provides for our needs and supplies the increase.

In 2 Corinthians 9:6–11 (NIV), Paul encourages the church to give willingly, cheerfully, and generously, saying, "Whoever sows sparingly will also reap sparingly, and whoever sows generously will also reap generously" (v. 6). He instructs us to give from the heart, not reluctantly, for "God loves a cheerful giver" (v. 7). He explains that God wants to bless us "abundantly" so that we can "abound in every good work" (v. 8). God supplies and increases our "store of seed" (v. 10), that we might be "generous on every occasion" (v. 11).

> *"Give, and it will be given to you. A good measure, pressed down, shaken together and running over, will be poured into your lap."*
> Luke 6:38 NIV

PERSONAL APPLICATION:

Where do you abound in generosity? And in what area of your life do you find it difficult to give? Generosity comes in many forms. You can meet practical and physical needs, give your time or energy to help others, and even support various ministries and missions. You can also meet spiritual needs and sow into the lives of others on a personal level by helping to disciple or mentor young people and new believers.

Just as Mary wants to see her garden grow, and just as Martha's family helps Mary blossom into a happy, healthy child, you and I have the opportunity to sow into the lives of others. There is much you can do to partner with God to actively plant seeds for the Gospel through evangelism or tend tender shoots of faith through discipleship. Take this time to ask the Lord where and how to give generously of your time, energy, and gifts.

PRAYER FOR TODAY:

Dear Jesus, thank You for all the people who have poured out their time and resources so that I could grow as a Christian. I ask You now to show me how and where I can take part in actively planting and watering seeds of faith in the lives of others. Teach me to use all that You've given to me so that I might overflow to others. Please enlarge my heart and my vision for Your kingdom work so that I might give generously in these areas: [your prayer]. In Jesus' name, amen.

God is able to bless you abundantly, so that in all things at all times, having all that you need, you will abound in every good work.

2 CORINTHIANS 9:8 NIV

DAY 10
Branching Out

As each part does its own special work, it helps the other parts grow, so that the whole body is healthy and growing and full of love.

EPHESIANS 4:16 NLT

[Dickon] told her what [the seeds] looked like when they were flowers; he told her how to plant them, and watch them, and feed and water them.

(CHAPTER 10)

Mary's discovery of the secret garden means she has something interesting and important to do each day. Whereas she used to feel languid and hot, tired and listless, she is now alive and curious and busy. Mary has a place where she fits, a job to do, and a purpose. Her days, which used to be dull and boring, are satisfying and full. She's an "odd, determined little person" who now has "something interesting to be determined about."

Mary becomes "very much absorbed" as she works and digs and pulls up weeds, "only becoming more pleased with her work every hour instead of tiring of it." She does everything she can to give her garden a chance to grow, clearing spaces around the new little shoots and dreaming of what it will look like when the garden begins to bloom. But as she works, Mary instinctively knows there is only so much she can do on her own. She needs help.

In her quest to help her garden grow and bloom, Mary visits with Ben Weatherstaff and peppers him with questions about gardening, planting, and how to tell if rose-bushes are "dead or alive." Next, when Dickon brings Mary the gardening tools and packets of seeds, he teaches her what the seeds will look like "when they [are] flowers" and how to "plant them, and watch them, and feed and water them." He even offers to help: "I'll plant them for thee myself. Where is tha' garden?" Mary decides to trust him with her secret and brings him into the garden.

Just as Mary asks for advice and help in the secret garden, we also need other believers who can guide our steps, provide us with spiritual tools, and encourage our efforts as we walk with Jesus. There is much we can do on our own, such as reading the Bible, praying, and attending church regularly. But when we allow other believers to step into our lives in an authentic way, they can help us explore God's direction, purpose, and calling for our lives. They can also teach us how to apply God's Word, model for us how to pray and follow Jesus, and help us develop practical skills for planting seeds of faith in others.

In Acts 18 (NIV), we read that Apollos was "a learned man, with a thorough knowledge of the Scriptures" (v. 24). However, though he had been "instructed in the way of the Lord" and "spoke with great fervor and taught about Jesus accurately," he only knew about the "baptism of John" (v. 25). Apollos had a lot of information, but he didn't have the full picture yet. When Priscilla and Aquila heard him speak in the synagogue, they "invited him to their home and explained to him the way of God more adequately" (v. 26). As a result of their teaching and equipping, Apollos made an enormous impact for the kingdom of God!

And he gave the apostles, the prophets,
the evangelists, the shepherds and teachers,
to equip the saints for the work of ministry,
for building up the body of Christ.
EPHESIANS 4:11–12 ESV

PERSONAL APPLICATION:

Throughout the New Testament, we see that discipleship is an essential part of our lives as believers. The first followers of Jesus didn't just evangelize and plant churches; they discipled and equipped the new believers so they could in turn continue to disciple and equip others. Every Christian needs ongoing discipleship, and every Christian is called to continually pour into others.

Do you want to go deeper in your walk with God? Do you desire to encourage others in their fledgling faith? Start praying today for a godly mentor for yourself, no matter what stage of life you're in. And keep your eyes open for opportunities to share with younger believers the tools you've been given and the "packets" of wisdom you've gathered thus far.

PRAYER FOR TODAY:

Lord, I want to grow in my faith, plant seeds of faith in others, and help build Your glorious kingdom. I know I need to be encouraged, challenged, and corrected in the practical parts of my daily walk. Please lead me to mature godly people who can help me do that. Help me remain authentic and open with the people I trust so I can receive prayer and accountability. I also desire to help others grow in their faith. Show me how I can help build up and equip these believers in my life: [specific names]. In Jesus' name, amen.

Let the wise hear and increase in learning, and the one who understands obtain guidance.

PROVERBS 1:5 ESV

ᴅAY 11
Still Wick

*"They are like trees planted
along a riverbank, with roots
that reach deep into the water."*

JEREMIAH 17:8 NLT

Mistress Mary always felt that however many years she lived she should never forget that first morning when her garden began to grow.

(CHAPTER II)

After ten years of neglect, the rosebushes and plants in the secret garden have grown into a "lovely gray tangle." Mary is desperate to find out if the rosebushes will bloom again. As Dickon stands inside the garden for the first time, looking around him in wonder, Mary puts her hand on his arm, asking tremulously if the roses are "all dead." With his expert eye, Dickon touches "a shoot" which looks "brownish green instead of hard, dry gray." He looks around and says, "Eh! No! Not them—not all of 'em!"

With hopeful delight, Mary watches as Dickon then begins to make small cuts in the dry, gray branches, showing her which rosebushes are still alive—or "wick." Though there's "lots o' dead wood as ought to be cut out," they find plenty of new growth. Dickon explains that while the most delicate roses have died, "th' strongest ones has fair thrived." One "lifeless-looking" branch looks like it's "dead wood," but when he cuts into it—"down to th' root"—there's still "green in that wood yet."

They eagerly go "from bush to bush and from tree to tree," clearing away dead branches, discovering new growth, and digging around the roots to "let the air in." When Dickon sees Mary's "own little clearings round the pale green points" all around the garden, he praises her and asks her why she did it. She says, "They were so little, and the grass was so thick and strong, and they looked as if they had no room to breathe."

Do you feel dry, brittle, or lifeless? Do you think your time of abundance, fruitfulness, and bloom is over? It's not! God is not done! God still has a plan for your life. You are still wick! You are worthwhile. You have good things to offer to others. Even though you may have been pruned back, you *will* bloom again! And in the areas that look gray, dead, or hopeless, remember that the same resurrection power that brought Jesus back from the dead is the same "incomparably great power" that's at work in you (Ephesians 1:19 NIV).

In 1 Kings 19 (NIV), the prophet Elijah ran away to the wilderness in despair. After years of drought and famine and warning the people of Israel to turn away from idols and back to God, he thought there was no hope left. He was so discouraged that he prayed for the Lord to let him die, but God sent an angel to tell him this instead: "Get up and eat, for the journey is too much for you" (v. 7). The Lord revealed Himself to Elijah in a radical way that day, gave him specific instructions to follow, and told him that there were seven thousand people in Israel who still followed God (v. 18). The Lord had more work for Elijah to do!

"Even to your old age and gray hairs I
am he, I am he who will sustain you.
I have made you and I will carry you;
I will sustain you and I will rescue you."

Isaiah 46:4 niv

———————◆◆———————

PERSONAL APPLICATION:

Dickon is "very strong and clever with his knife and [knows] how to cut the dry and dead wood away, and [can] tell when an unpromising bough or twig" still has "green life in it." To a far greater degree, God knows just when and what to prune and trim in your life so that you can bear more fruit. If you're in a season of pruning, remember this: God "prunes the branches that do bear fruit so they will produce even more" (John 15:2 nlt).

In the secret garden, it's the strongest roses that "fair thrived," but they were in dire need of care and attention. And the same is true for you. If you feel like that long-forgotten garden, invite Jesus to step in like a gentle gardener and tend to the wild, tangled places of your heart. Ask Him to water your thirsty soul and revive your weary heart. Ask Him to make you like a tree with its roots planted by a stream, that you might produce fruit in *every* season (Jeremiah 17:8, emphasis mine).

PRAYER FOR TODAY:

Lord, thank You for sustaining me in every season. I confess that I often neglect the care and keeping of my heart. I want to actively nourish, fertilize, and grow my faith and make more room for You to work in my life. Show me what needs to be pruned back and cleared away. Please pour out Your Spirit on me in a new way. Thank You for reminding me that I'm still "wick" and that You still have work for me to do. In the areas where I feel dry and brittle, please renew my strength: [your request]. In Jesus' name, amen.

Now all glory to God, who is able, through his mighty power at work within us, to accomplish infinitely more than we might ask or think.

EPHESIANS 3:20 NLT

Ⓓay 12
A Bit of Earth

"If you ask anything in My name, I will do it."

John 14:14 NKJV

*"Might I," quavered Mary,
"might I have a bit of earth?"*
(CHAPTER 12)

When Mary runs in from the garden, rosy-cheeked and windblown, expecting to eat her dinner and run back to Dickon, she learns that Mr. Craven wants to see her. Immediately, "all the pink" leaves her cheeks, her heart begins to "thump," and she becomes a "stiff, plain, silent child again." When they meet, she stands before him, "twisting her thin hands together." But as they talk, Mary is given a rare opportunity to ask for something she wants very much.

Though Mr. Craven says he cannot give Mary his own "time or attention" because he is "too ill, and wretched and distracted," he does want her "to be happy and comfortable." Thanks to Mrs. Sowerby's wise suggestion, he decides to forgo a governess for the time being and allow Mary plenty of "fresh air and freedom and running about." He agrees that she needs to get stronger and healthier before she starts her lessons, and he tells her to "play out of doors," explore the grounds, and amuse herself as much as she likes.

Before sending her away, he asks one more question:

"Is there anything you want?" He mentions toys, books, and dolls, but there is only one thing Mary truly wants: "a bit of earth" for her garden, "to plant seeds in—to make things grow—to see them come alive." When she summons up the courage to ask for what she wants, Mr. Craven's eyes soften and he tells her she can have "as much earth" as she wants. He says, "When you see a bit of earth you want. . .take it, child, and make it come alive."

If a broken man like Mr. Craven can so easily give Mary a plot of earth on his vast estate, just think what God, the Creator of the universe, can do for you! Your heavenly Father has resources beyond your imagination. Everything on the earth is His; He owns the cattle on a thousand hills (Psalm 50:10). And He invites His people to come to Him— with anything and everything: "If you ask anything in My name, I will do it" (John 14:14 NKJV). God isn't a genie in a bottle, but He delights in giving good gifts to His children when they ask (Matthew 7:11)!

Hebrews 4:16 (NKJV) says, "Let us therefore come boldly to the throne of grace, that we may obtain mercy and find grace to help in time of need." As a follower of Christ, you now have access to God's throne of grace. As you come before Him with a humble heart, asking for His will to be done, don't be bashful—and don't leave anything out. Go to God with your eager, anxious requests. Run to Him freely and quickly with your every need, with your greatest fears, and with your wildest dreams. Ask Him to expand your territory and give you a "bit of earth" to tend.

"If you then, who are evil, know how to give good gifts to your children, how much more will your Father who is in heaven give good things to those who ask him!"

MATTHEW 7:11 ESV

PERSONAL APPLICATION:

Mr. Craven invites Mary to find a garden plot she likes, "take it," and "make it come alive." As you pray about where God wants you to live and serve, ask Him to show you the specific place of personal ministry where He wants you to share your faith, tend hearts, and help others "come alive" in Christ. You are "God's handiwork, created in Christ Jesus to do good works, which God prepared in advance for [you] to do" (Ephesians 2:10 NIV).

Is there a situation or prayer request on your heart that seems impossible? Have you lacked the courage to pray with confidence about certain matters? If so, stop now and write down a list of "bold prayers." Come before the Lord and humbly ask, in the name of Jesus, for God's will to be done in each situation. Ask Him to do something only He can do. Be specific. Be persistent. And watch what He will do.

PRAYER FOR TODAY:

Lord God, thank You for inviting me to come boldly to Your throne of grace. I lift to You now the prayer requests that seem too big. I bring before You the areas where my own fears and weaknesses hold me back; the healing, the help, and the provision that I need; and the places where I lack the courage and boldness to step out and live on mission for You. Most of all, I humbly ask You to work in a miraculous way in these difficult situations and relationships: [your prayer]. In Jesus' powerful name, amen.

Let us therefore come boldly to the throne of grace, that we may obtain mercy and find grace to help in time of need.

HEBREWS 4:16 NKJV

Ｄay 13
Rainy Day Delays

He makes me lie down in green pastures. He leads me beside still waters.

PSALM 23:2 ESV

"[The spring] is the sun shining on the rain and the rain falling on the sunshine, and things pushing up and working under the earth."
(CHAPTER 13)

After meeting Dickon and getting her new gardening tools and seed packets, Mary can't wait to go back to the garden again. She goes to sleep "looking forward" to the next day, but unfortunately, "you never know what the weather will do in Yorkshire, particularly in the springtime." Mary wakes up in the night to the sound of rain "beating with heavy drops against her window." And it's not just a light drizzle—the rain is "pouring down in torrents."

Mary's response is no surprise: She sits up in bed, feeling "miserable and angry," and says, "The rain is as contrary as I ever was. . . . It came because it knew I did not want it." Throwing herself back on her pillow, she buries her face. She doesn't cry, but she lies there actively hating "the sound of the heavily beating rain" and the "wuthering" wind. But as she tosses and turns on her bed, she begins to distinguish the mournful sounds of the storm from something else—the sound of someone crying.

The crying she hears leads Mary to another part of the house, where she meets her cousin Colin, whom she has never met or even heard of. As they become acquainted there in the middle of the night, Colin talks about his poor health, his father who hardly sees him, and his mother who died. He even shows her a portrait of his mother. Mary speaks of India, living at Misselthwaite, and the hidden garden. It's the beginning of a special bond between the two cousins and the start of a greater work of healing than either of them could ever imagine.

It's easy to understand Mary's disappointment and irritation when her plans in the garden with Dickon are spoiled, but this chapter points to an important lesson: sometimes the delays we experience are for a greater purpose. When our plans change, our first reaction is often frustration, especially if we feel as though we're finally gaining momentum or making progress; but if we will stop and listen, God often has something to say in the pause. God-ordained stops are for a reason—they give us time to rest and listen, and they give Him time to move and work.

Pauses are part of God's design for the well-being of His people. After all His work of creation, God rested on the seventh day from all His work and blessed it and sanctified it (Genesis 2:2–3). In the wilderness, God told the Israelites to gather manna for six days and rest on the seventh (Exodus 16:26). And in the Ten Commandments, God gave this command: "Remember the sabbath day, to keep it holy" (Exodus 20:8 KJV). Throughout the

Bible, the Sabbath is part of the weekly rhythm of life, a day set aside for rest and worship. Today, keeping the Sabbath is still part of God's good plans for His people.

Jesus said to them, "The Sabbath was made for man, and not man for the Sabbath."

MARK 2:27 NASB

---◆◆◆---

PERSONAL APPLICATION:

Are you taking advantage of God's intended rests, or do you need to slow down and reprioritize? In Exodus 16, God said no manna would fall on the Sabbath, but some people still went out to try to gather some. In Psalm 23, the psalmist says, "He *makes* me lie down in green pastures" (Psalm 23:2 ESV, emphasis added). These examples point to the fact that rest isn't something we willingly do. But the Sabbath is an incredibly loving commandment. It's God's design for His people to rest, be still, and prepare for the week ahead. It's not a punishment; it's a gift!

Just as Mary made new discoveries on a dreary, rainy day—including Colin's cry in the corridor—God can use delays and changes of pace to show us new things and speak in ways we couldn't hear if we were busy with our usual routines. The next time you're ill or your plans get canceled, think of it as an opportunity instead of an inconvenience and ask the Lord to reveal His plans and purposes. There may be something He wants to say that you need to hear.

PRAYER FOR TODAY

Lord Jesus, thank You for the gift of rest and a weekly Sabbath. Help me to work diligently when it's time to do my work and chores, and help me to set everything down when it's time to rest. I want to learn to be still and hear Your voice above the storm of busyness that frequently takes over my day. In the times when I'm frustrated by delays, help me remember that You often work in the pauses. I ask for Your help to set aside these distractions that keep me from true rest: [your prayer]. In Jesus' name, amen.

"Come to me, all who labor and are heavy laden, and I will give you rest."

MATTHEW 11:28 ESV

DAY 14
Let the Light In

The people who walked in darkness
have seen a great light; those who
dwelt in a land of deep darkness,
on them has light shone.

ISAIAH 9:2 ESV

"See here," [Mary] said. "Don't let us talk about dying; I don't like it. Let us talk about living."
(CHAPTER 14)

As Mary becomes acquainted with Colin, it's clear that most of what's wrong with Colin is not physical. Sadly, he's the product of the heartache that surrounded his birth—when his mother died and his father "went off his head," when there was "enough trouble and raging in th' house to set any child wrong." Since then, Colin has been neglected by his father, spoiled by the staff, and left to his own dark, anxious thoughts.

What's more, Colin has been treated like an invalid for so long that he's come to believe he is one. His mind is tangled with thoughts of illness and death; his emotions are crowded with anxiety and fear; and his heart is over-grown with selfishness and conceit. When Mary comes on the scene, she brings with her an entirely new narrative. She doesn't like that he talks about dying, and says that if people wanted her to die—she "wouldn't" do it. She suggests they stop talking about dying and "talk about living" instead.

When Mary changes the subject from death to life, it's truly "the best thing she could have said." She tells Colin stories about Dickon, the moor, the cottage with fourteen people, and the Sowerby children who seem to get "fat on the moor grass like the wild ponies." She paints word pictures of the plants and gardens that are waking up with the spring. Soon enough, Colin forgets all about his "weak back" and they both "laugh over nothings as children will when they are happy together."

Colin's story provides a picture of what it looks like to live life in the shadows—with only fear, isolation, and hopelessness as our daily companions. Only Jesus can shine a light into the low valleys of our hearts and minds and break us free from the heavy burdens we carry. Only Jesus can redeem our failures, heal our wounds, and untangle our messes. And only Jesus has the power to bring a person out from spiritual darkness and into the light, from death to life.

In Isaiah 9:2, Isaiah prophesied that a great light would come into this dark world, to set the captives free from the shackles of sin and death. And in Matthew 4:16 (ESV), when Jesus was born, it came to pass: "The people dwelling in darkness have seen a great light, and for those dwelling in the region and shadow of death, on them a light has dawned." Jesus is the Light of the world (John 8:12) who came to set us free from the penalty of sin and death. Anyone who follows Him will no longer walk in darkness but will receive eternal life and walk in the light.

Again Jesus spoke to them, saying,
"I am the light of the world. Whoever
follows me will not walk in darkness,
but will have the light of life."

JOHN 8:12 ESV

PERSONAL APPLICATION:

Do you know people who are sitting in the shadows? Who are longing for joy but haven't found it yet? God is calling you to share the Gospel of Christ with the people you meet each day who do not yet know Him: "How, then, can they call on the one they have not believed in? And how can they believe in the one of whom they have not heard? And how can they hear without someone preaching to them?" (Romans 10:14 NIV).

There are others who know and love Jesus but are weary and in great need of refreshment. As you pray today, ask Jesus to show you how to bring His light and hope to fellow believers who are walking alone or in a low valley. Step in with a fresh dose of encouragement and hope. If you are the one who is struggling, reach out to a trusted friend for prayer today.

PRAYER FOR TODAY:

Jesus, thank You for piercing through the darkness of this world with Your great love. Thank You for pursuing me, for loving me, and for saving me. Please help me to bring the Good News of Jesus into the lives of my friends, neighbors, coworkers, and family members. Lead me to those people who are sitting in darkness and need to know You. In the times when I feel anxious and overwhelmed, help me claim Your promises and place my worries in Your hands. Please shine Your light on this specific area of my life where I need a new way of looking at things: [your prayer]. In Jesus' name, amen.

"How beautiful are the feet of those who bring good news!"

ROMANS 10:15 NIV

ᴰAY 15
Bursting with Joy

*Sing to the L*ᴏʀᴅ*; praise his name. Each day proclaim the good news that he saves.*

Pꜱᴀʟᴍ 96:2 ɴʟᴛ

"When th' sun did jump up, th' moor went mad for joy, an' I was in the midst of th' heather, an' I run like mad myself, shoutin' an' singin'."
(CHAPTER 15)

After a week of rain, Mary wakes up "very early" one morning to the sun "pouring in slanting rays through the blinds." There is "something so joyous in the sight of it" that she jumps out of bed and opens the window to let in "a great waft of fresh, scented air." As Mary puts out her hand to feel the sun, she exclaims, "It's warm—warm!" She knows it will "make the green points push up and up and up, and. . .make the bulbs and roots work and struggle with all their might under the earth." She can't stay inside a moment longer and runs out to the garden.

Outside, she clasps her hands "for pure joy," feeling as if "she must flute and sing aloud herself." As she goes, she is overjoyed at the sight of things "sprouting and pushing out from the roots of clumps of plants." In the garden, Dickon, who was up before the sun, is just as excited as Mary. He tells her that as he came across the moor, all of nature was "workin' an' hummin' an' scratchin' an' pipin' an' nest-buildin' an' breathin' out scents"—and when it all went "mad for joy" as the sun came up, he ran "like mad" himself, "shoutin' an' singin'."

As they investigate all the nooks and corners of the garden, Mary and Dickon find ever so many "swelling leaf-buds on rose branches which had seemed dead" and "ten thousand new green points pushing through the mould." As they watch the robin "nest-buildin'," they settle on one common thought: the secret garden is too wonderful to keep to themselves. They believe Colin needs to visit because "he wouldn't be watchin' for lumps to grow on his back" if he could start "watchin' for buds to break on th' rose-bushes."

There's nothing quite as pleasurable as the abundant life in Christ—especially during times of renewed hope and revival. We experience fresh, healing breezes, tender new shoots of faith, sunshine falling on rain, and buds of hope. And when we see the fruit of God's handiwork on display, it feels as though our hearts might burst with "pure joy." As we brim over with His goodness, we can't help but invite our friends to know Him too.

The overwhelming joy of knowing Jesus is so wonderful that it's absolutely infectious. In John 1, word about Jesus spread rapidly. After Jesus' baptism, John the Baptist told two of his own disciples that Jesus was the Lamb of God. They followed after Jesus, and one of them, named Andrew, went and told his brother Simon (Peter) the good news: "We have found the Messiah" (John 1:41 ESV). The next day,

Jesus called Philip to come follow Him, and Philip went and told Nathanael he had found "him of whom Moses in the Law and also the prophets wrote" (John 1:45 ESV). The news continued to spread, and soon entire crowds followed Jesus everywhere He went!

> *Publish his glorious deeds among*
> *the nations. Tell everyone about*
> *the amazing things he does.*
>
> PSALM 96:3 NLT

PERSONAL APPLICATION:

Jesus' disciples couldn't help sharing about Him with others—and we are called to do the same. If you know about Jesus, it's most likely because someone told you about Him! As you experience the goodness of God, share it with someone else. Let your love for Him brim over into the lives of others. Share what you're reading in your devotions. Teach others how to read and enjoy the Bible. Hold hands and pray with friends.

Mary and Dickon helped care for the secret garden, but only God can make a garden grow. As you serve God and invest in spiritual "nest buildin'" in your church and community, remember Paul's encouragement: "I [Paul] planted the seed, Apollos watered it, but God has been making it grow" (1 Corinthians 3:6 NIV). Your job isn't to save people; your job is to plant and water seeds of faith—and allow God to do the rest.

PRAYER FOR TODAY:

Jesus, I praise You for all that You've done in my life and for the many people who have told me about You over the years. I want my relationship with You to burst forth with new life. Enlighten the eyes of my heart that I may know the hope to which You have called me, the riches of Your glorious inheritance, and Your incomparably great power at work in my life (Ephesians 1:18–19). Fill me anew with wonder at the beauty of Jesus. Help me to share the incredible joy of knowing You with these people: [specific names]. In Jesus' name, amen.

For I am not ashamed of the gospel, for it is the power of God for salvation to everyone who believes, to the Jew first and also to the Greek.

ROMANS 1:16 ESV

ᴅAY 16
Stormy Skies

*Let each of you look not only
to his own interests, but also
to the interests of others.*

PHILIPPIANS 2:4 ESV

*Everything was so nice that [Mary's] pleasure
began to crowd her anger out of her mind. . .
and her hard little heart grew quite warm.*
(CHAPTER 16)

In this chapter, Mary and Colin hit a rough patch in their friendship when they both think only of themselves and not of each other. It all starts when Mary, who is not "afraid of [Colin]" and is "not a self-sacrificing person," spends the entire morning outside and thoughtlessly runs back to the garden after her lunch without ever checking in on Colin. When Martha says he's been waiting anxiously for her all morning, Mary offhandedly says to tell him she "can't come and see him" because she's "very busy in the garden."

Upon returning to the house after an afternoon that was "even lovelier and busier than the morning," Mary can't wait to tell Colin all about it. However, her mood changes when Martha tells her that Colin is "nigh goin' into one o' his tantrums." Mary, who is "no more used to considering other people than Colin" and sees "no reason why an ill-tempered boy should interfere with the thing she like[s] best," storms off to see him. They argue fiercely, going toe to toe, until Colin orders her to leave and Mary says she's never coming back.

Back in her room, Mary discovers a box of gifts from Mr. Craven: colorful gardening books, several games, and a "beautiful little writing-case with a gold monogram on it and a gold pen and inkstand." Mary's "pleasure [begins] to crowd her anger out of her mind" and "her hard little heart [grows] quite warm." As she slows down and thinks about what's behind Colin's tantrums, she remembers his "hysterical hidden fear" about his back. She softens at the thought of him alone with his fears all day and decides to go see him the next morning after all.

When we are too caught up in our own interests and concerns, we sometimes overlook the needs of others. So often, we only see one side to a situation or quarrel—the part that affects us personally. But Philippians 2:4 (ESV) says, "Let each of you look not only to his own interests, but *also to the interests of others*" (emphasis added). This isn't easy to do, especially when we feel wronged; but if we will pray and ask God to soften our hearts, He will provide the change of perspective we need.

In Luke 10:29–37 (NIV), we see an example of selfishness versus selflessness: A priest and a Levite each passed by a man who had been attacked by robbers, stripped, beaten, and left "half dead" (v. 30). Each man crossed to the other side of the street and continued on his way, too busy and too self-involved to help. But when a Samaritan saw the man, "he took pity on him" (v. 33). He bandaged his wounds and took him to an inn and cared for him. He even paid extra so the man could stay longer and fully convalesce. The Samaritan set aside his own agenda and saw the wounded man as a person in need, rather than as an inconvenience or interruption.

Finally, all of you, be like-minded,
be sympathetic, love one another,
be compassionate and humble.

1 PETER 3:8 NIV

PERSONAL APPLICATION:

Noticing the needs of others involves slowing down and paying attention. When we just think of ourselves, we often miss the bigger picture. We need special insight from the Lord to see what's below the surface of tense conversations and tricky relationships. Putting the interests of others first doesn't mean we let people walk all over us, but it does mean that we actively consider their thoughts, feelings, and experiences.

Where in your life do you see a tendency toward self-ishness? Take time to pray over any recent conversations that might need smoothing over. If you're prone to stormy emotions or hasty words, ask God to help you navigate difficult situations with grace and a soft answer (Proverbs 15:1). And take note of the times when you're more likely to miss certain signals from other people—either because you're in a rush, focused on your own concerns, or feeling stressed.

PRAYER FOR TODAY:

Lord Jesus, I confess that I tend to get caught up in my own worries and concerns and don't always notice the people around me. I can get so busy that I fail to notice the needs of others. I sometimes get tense and short tempered. Work in my heart and teach me to slow down, listen carefully, and treat others with compassion and humility. Help me to see where people are at and meet them there. Please soften my heart and show me any underlying issues in these situations or relationships: [your prayer]. In Jesus' name, amen.

My dear brothers and sisters, take note of this: Everyone should be quick to listen, slow to speak and slow to become angry.

JAMES 1:19 NIV

DAY 17
Every Thought Captive

*We demolish arguments and
every pretension that sets itself
up against the knowledge of God,
and we take captive every thought
to make it obedient to Christ.*

2 CORINTHIANS 10:5 NIV

If [Colin] had ever had anyone to talk to about his secret terrors. . .he would have found out that most of his fright and illness was created by himself.

(CHAPTER 17)

In this chapter, Mary steps in and finally breaks through the barrier that holds Colin back from life, hope, and joy—his fear of developing a "lump" on his back. The breakthrough happens when Mary awakens in the night to the "dreadful" sound of someone "screaming and crying in a horrible way." When she realizes it's Colin "having one of those tantrums" the nurse calls "hysterics," she runs straight to his room, slaps open the door, and shouts at him to stop.

Mary threatens to scream even "louder" if he screams again, saying that "hysterics" are "half that ails" him. Finally, he chokes out the reason for his tantrum: "I felt the lump—I felt it. . . . I shall have a hunch on my back and then I shall die." Mary contradicts him "fiercely," saying he *didn't* feel a lump: "There's nothing the matter with your horrid back—nothing but hysterics!" And so, while Colin holds his breath, Mary examines his "poor thin back" once and for all.

When Mary finds only "backbone lumps" and the nurse confirms it and provides further assurances, "great tears [stream] down his face and wet the pillow," and a "curious great relief" comes over him. He's never talked to anyone "about his secret terrors" or "dared to let himself ask questions." He's lived in a "huge closed house, breathing an atmosphere heavy with the fears of people who were most of them ignorant." He's "lain and thought of himself and his aches and weariness for hours and days and months and years," trapped in a prison of fear. It's only when he shares his hidden thoughts with Mary that he is set free from years of inner turmoil.

Our "secret terrors" grow and fester when we stew on them and keep them hidden. When the lies we believe become overgrown, they begin to take over, crowding out rational thought and choking our joy. Sometimes it even feels as though our thoughts have taken *us* captive! But the Bible teaches us that we *can* control our thoughts and "take captive every thought to make it obedient to Christ" (2 Corinthians 10:5 NIV). Taking control of your thoughts and bringing them in line with the truth of God's Word will strengthen you to stand firm against anything that threatens to steal the peace and freedom you have in Christ.

Jesus came to set us free from anything that has power over us—sin, temptation, idolatry, fear, and every other thing that might enslave us. Galatians 5:1 (NIV) says, "It is for freedom that Christ has set us free. Stand firm, then, and do not let yourselves be burdened again by a yoke of slavery." In order to do that, it's crucial that we not only bring everything to Jesus and into the light but also share our struggles with one another: "Therefore, confess your sins to one another and pray for one another, that you may be healed" (James 5:16 ESV). We need trustworthy Christian friends who can pray for us, encourage us, and keep us accountable.

> *The weapons we fight with are not the weapons of the world. On the contrary, they have divine power to demolish strongholds.*
>
> 2 CORINTHIANS 10:4 NIV

PERSONAL APPLICATION:

Many of the battles we face stem from the thoughts we harbor and allow to reign in our minds and in our imaginations. If you want to experience victory in the areas of temptation, fear, and anxiety, start by tending to your thought life. Ask the Lord to help you diligently weed out and bring to Jesus any thought that runs contrary to His Word.

If you feel like you're fighting a losing battle, make sure you're suited up! Ephesians 6:11–18 instructs us to put on the *full* armor of God: the belt of truth, the breastplate of righteousness, the shoes of the gospel of peace, the shield of faith, the helmet of salvation, and the sword of the Spirit. Use a Bible commentary or study guide to help you learn how to utilize each piece of your God-given spiritual armor. Finally, share your struggles with at least one trusted Christian believer and ask for prayer. Remember, you are not in this battle alone!

PRAYER FOR TODAY:

Lord Jesus, I recognize that my mind often plays and replays information, ideas, and scenes that aren't healthy or profitable. Help me open up to other Christians and bring my burdens into the light, rather than hiding them or stewing on them. Grant me the wisdom and discernment I need to spot any thought pattern that does not square up with the Bible and might cause me to stumble or become fearful or depressed. I want to experience more freedom and victory in You. In my thought life, please show me the lies I've believed in these difficult areas: [your prayer]. In Jesus' name, amen.

Put on the whole armor of God, that you may be able to stand against the wiles of the devil.
EPHESIANS 6:11 NKJV

DAY 18
Shared Sweetness

For we are to God the pleasing aroma of Christ among those who are being saved and those who are perishing.

2 CORINTHIANS 2:15 NIV

"You smell like flowers and—and fresh things," [Colin] cried out quite joyously. "What is it you smell of? It's cool and warm and sweet all at the same time."
(CHAPTER 18)

The day after his tantrum, Colin asks if Mary will "please" come visit him—a word he never normally uses. Mary tells him she's going outside first, but she promises she "won't be long," that it's "something about the garden." His "whole face" brightens and "a little color" comes into his pale face as he tells Mary that he dreamed he was standing in the garden: "In a place all filled with trembling little green leaves. . .and birds on nests everywhere."

In the garden, Mary sits on the grass with Dickon and his animals, taking in the beautiful sights, smells, and sounds all around. She tells Dickon about Colin's tantrum, and he declares, "We mun get him out here—we mun get him watchin' an listenin' an' sniffin' up th' air an' get him just soaked through wi' sunshine." And then, though it's "hard to go away and leave it all," Mary keeps her word and goes back inside to Colin, bringing the garden and spring with her.

Colin sniffs curiously at her, crying out "quite joyously" that she smells "like flowers and—and fresh things." He describes the scent as "cool and warm and sweet all at the same time," which Mary says is "th' wind from th' moor." She talks "broad Yorkshire" to him, which makes them both laugh until the room echoes. She tells him about "Dickon and Captain and Soot and Nut and Shell and the pony whose name [is] Jump." Colin apologizes for the way he spoke about Dickon when he was angry, and Mary assures him that Dickon is planning to come visit him soon. Finally—with "solemn excitement"—Mary shares with Colin the sweetest news of all: she's found the secret garden.

Just as Mary brought the sweet scent of the garden with her into Colin's room, your life carries the sweet fragrance of knowing and loving Jesus to the people you meet each day. As you spend time with Him and in the Word, allowing the Holy Spirit to move and work in your heart, the work of the Lord in your life will naturally become evident to others. It will be like a sweet fragrance to the world around you: "We are to God the pleasing aroma of Christ among those who are being saved and those who are perishing" (2 Corinthians 2:15 NIV).

In the Old Testament, when Moses received the Ten Commandments, everyone knew he had been with God: "Now it was so, when Moses came down from Mount Sinai . . .his face shone while he talked with Him" (Exodus 34:29 NKJV). In fact, the light from Moses' face was so bright, he covered it with a veil when he was with the people. The time

Moses spent sitting with God—listening to Him, receiving His instructions, and worshipping Him—had a glorious effect: his very face reflected God's glory! May the same be true for you and for me.

In your presence there is fullness of joy;
at your right hand are pleasures forevermore.
PSALM 16:11 ESV

PERSONAL APPLICATION:

Mary smelled like the wind off the moor and "flowers. . . and fresh things" because she spent time in the outdoors. If we want our faces and lives to become radiant with the joy of knowing and following Jesus, we need to sit "in the garden" with Him, basking in His love. We need to immerse ourselves in His Word and devote ourselves to worship and adoration. Gazing at Him from afar won't do it; we need to meet Him face-to-face.

In Acts 4:13 (NIV), when the religious leaders "saw the courage of Peter and John and realized that they were unschooled, ordinary men, they were astonished and they took note that these men had been with Jesus." There is nothing quite so captivating or contagious as the joy that comes from a life lived in close relationship with Jesus. If you want to be Christ's ambassador to the people in your life, make time this week to sit in His presence—enjoying

Him and learning from Him. When people meet you, they will *know* you've been with Jesus!

PRAYER FOR TODAY:

Jesus, thank You for inviting me to come near to sit with You. I want to take this time to be still before You and enjoy Your presence. Please help me quiet my mind and heart so I can hear the still, small voice of the Holy Spirit. May my worship of You be like a sweet fragrance before You. May my time in Your Word produce fruit. I want to bring You with me into my everyday life and shine for You. Please make my life a reflection of Your glory and Your goodness to these people: [specific names]. In Jesus' name, amen.

They were astonished and they took note that these men had been with Jesus.

ACTS 4:13 NIV

DAY 19
Little Lambs

"I lay down My life for the sheep."
JOHN 10:15 NKJV

*It was not the first motherless lamb [Dickon]
had found and he knew what to do with it.*
(CHAPTER 19)

One morning, Colin wakes up smiling and feeling "curiously comfortable." As he stretches "his limbs luxuriously," it's as if "tight strings which had held him" have "loosened themselves and let him go." When Mary comes, bringing with her a "waft of fresh air full of the scent of the morning," he asks her to open the window. He lies back to breathe in "long breaths" of the fresh moor air, feeling that "something quite new and delightful [is] happening to him."

Mary describes the secret garden with its "uncurling" flowers and busy nesting birds, and she tells Colin about the motherless newborn lamb Dickon found on the moor: "A lamb—a lamb! A living lamb who lay on your lap like a baby!" When Dickon arrives, he has the newborn lamb in his arms, the little red fox trotting beside him, Nut and Soot on either shoulder, and Shell "peep[ing] out of his coat pocket." Colin slowly sits up and stares and stares— "as he had stared when he first saw Mary"—except this is "a stare of wonder and delight." Dickon comes forward and lays the lamb on Colin's lap, pulls out a bottle, and begins to feed the hungry lamb.

As questions "[pour] forth," Dickon tells Colin and Mary how he heard the "weak bleatin'" of a hungry lamb on the moor "just as the sun was rising three mornings" before and set off "searchin'" for it. He looked and looked, going in and out among the bushes and "round an' round." At last, he found it by a rock on "top o' th' moor." It was not the first motherless lamb he'd found, and "he knew what to do with it." He climbed up to get it, took it to the cottage "wrapped in his jacket," and fed it by the fire. Colin and Mary are both amazed at his story—and "Dickon an' his creatures" bring joy to two more motherless children.

Dickon's description of how he searched and searched until he found the lost lamb provides a beautiful picture of the heart of Jesus for lost souls. Throughout the Bible, God is referred to as a loving Shepherd and His people as sheep. "He tends his flock like a shepherd: He gathers the lambs in his arms and carries them close to his heart." (Isaiah 40:11 NIV). In John 10:14 (NIV), Jesus said, "I am the good shepherd." And in Mark 6:34, we read that Jesus had compassion on the crowds because He saw they were like sheep without a shepherd.

Isaiah 53:6 (NIV) tells us that every person is like a sheep that has gone its own way: "We all, like sheep, have gone astray, each of us has turned to our own way; and the LORD has laid on him the iniquity of us all." The beauty of the Gospel is this: Jesus said, "I lay down My life for the sheep" (John 10:15 NKJV). Jesus not only gave His life for us, but He also actively seeks out those who are lost, like a shepherd looking for one lost sheep: "When he finds it, he joyfully puts it on his shoulders and goes home" (Luke 15:5–6 NIV). And when one person repents and is saved, all of heaven rejoices (Luke 15:7)!

> *"I tell you that in the same way there will be more rejoicing in heaven over one sinner who repents than over ninety-nine righteous persons who do not need to repent."*
>
> LUKE 15:7 NIV

PERSONAL APPLICATION:

When you gave your life to Christ, you became a child of God. He delights in you and will lead you, carry you, and nurture you. He is *your* Good Shepherd. If you need to be fed, carried, or helped, cry out to Jesus. If you feel lost or alone, ask Him to hold you close to His heart. Like Dickon with the lost little lamb, He knows just what you need.

Is there someone on your heart who seems out of reach or too far gone? Don't think for a moment that Jesus has given up on that person. Jesus is in the business of pursuing the lost—no matter how far they've wandered. Your part is to pray and never give up (Luke 18:1). The prayers of a righteous person are powerful and effective (James 5:16).

PRAYER FOR TODAY:

Lord Jesus, thank You for dying for me and for taking away my sins. I love You with all my heart. Thank You for gathering me in Your arms and carrying me close to Your heart. Please lead me and guide me. Feed me and nourish me so I can thrive and grow. And help me to mature in my faith and actively share Your love with others. I ask You to please seek out and bring home these people who are wandering: [specific names]. In Jesus' name, amen.

———————◆◆———————

He tends his flock like a shepherd:
He gathers the lambs in his arms and
carries them close to his heart; he
gently leads those that have young.

ISAIAH 40:11 NIV

DAY 20
Taste and See

*Oh, taste and see that
the LORD is good!*

PSALM 34:8 ESV

"I was thinking that I've really never seen [the springtime] before. I scarcely ever went out and when I did go I never looked at it."
(CHAPTER 20)

Colin can't wait to get outside and see springtime and the secret garden with his own eyes. When he first ventures outside in his wheelchair with Dickon and Mary, his big eyes seem to be "listening." He breathes in the "wild clear scented sweetness" of the wind and looks with "eager curiousness" at the places he's heard so much about: the path where Mary used to "walk up and down and wonder and wonder," the ivy wall where the robin "perched on the little heap of earth" and showed her the key, and the hidden door under the "hanging green curtain" of ivy.

At the door of the secret garden, Colin leans back in his chair and covers his eyes as Dickon pushes him inside "with one strong, steady, splendid push." Then he uncovers his eyes and looks "round and round and round," trying to take it all in. Now that it's spring, the "fair green veil of tender little leaves" has crept over everything, and "here and there everywhere [are] touches or splashes of gold and purple and white." The trees are "showing pink and snow above his head," and there's a "fluttering of wings and faint sweet pipes and humming and scents and scents."

All of Mary's and Dickon's descriptions have, in reality, only given Colin a partial understanding of the overwhelming wonder of the secret garden. No words or drawings could possibly do it justice or capture its beauty. Nothing compares to the joy of seeing it for himself. It's only when he's in the garden, experiencing it in person, that he truly understands everything he's been told about its charm and mystery. Once he sees it, his heart overflows with joy and hope: "I shall get well! And I shall live forever and ever and ever!"

Colin's experience of the secret garden paints a picture for us of the vast difference between hearing *about* Jesus and actually experiencing His goodness for ourselves. Psalm 34:8 (ESV) gives us this invitation to truly know God in a tangible, personal way: "Oh, taste and see that the LORD is good!" If we only have secondhand knowledge of Jesus, then we only get to know Him on the surface. But when we step into a saving relationship with Him, we get to know Him intimately—in all His glorious wonder.

God is not far-off or unreachable. He is not on a flaming mountaintop, concealed by a cloud, or hidden in a burning bush. He revealed Himself to people throughout the Bible in a variety of ways. Best of all, God sent His Son, Jesus, in bodily form so that we could see and *know* Him in a personal way: "He is the image of the invisible God, the firstborn of all creation" (Colossians 1:15 ESV). He is the "Word became flesh" that came and "dwelt among us" so that we might see "his glory, glory as of the only Son from the Father, full of grace and truth" (John 1:14 ESV). He is our Immanuel, "God *with* us" (Matthew 1:23 NKJV, emphasis added).

> *"Behold, the virgin shall be with child, and*
> *bear a Son, and they shall call His name*
> *Immanuel," which is translated, "God with us."*
> MATTHEW 1:23 NKJV

PERSONAL APPLICATION:

In John 20, Thomas needed to see for himself that Jesus had risen from the dead—and Jesus did not turn him away. He invited Thomas to touch His wounds, that he might *know* that Jesus had died and truly was alive again. Thomas's story was recorded for our benefit! Because of Thomas's testimony and so many others, we too can taste and see that the Lord is who He says He is, even though we have not seen Jesus in person.

Do you feel as though you've lost your sense of wonder? Do you long to experience the "wild clear scented sweetness" of Jesus' love all over again? We all go through valleys and droughts, but the Lord can revive our hearts in any season. If you are in need of spiritual renewal, stop now and ask the Lord to bring you into a season of personal revival. Your outward circumstances may not change, but your inner life can blossom with joy again. And if you've only heard about Jesus but want to know more about Him and experience His loving-kindness for yourself, I invite you to turn to the Special Invitation on page 194 to learn more.

PRAYER FOR TODAY:

Lord, I want to experience the wonder of knowing You personally all over again. Thank You for coming to earth, Jesus, so that I could know God fully. Your presence is like stepping into a garden and feeling the sun shine down on me. I want to learn from You and be transformed into Your likeness. I don't want to just know about You—I want to know You. Please revive my heart and help me "taste and see" that You are good in this area of my life: [your request]. In Jesus' name, amen.

Though you have not seen him, you love him. Though you do not now see him, you believe in him and rejoice with joy that is inexpressible and filled with glory.

1 PETER 1:8 ESV

DAY 21
A Place to Grow

The whole body, joined and held together by every joint with which it is equipped, when each part is working properly, makes the body grow so that it builds itself up in love.

EPHESIANS 4:16 ESV

*"I'm going to see everything grow here.
I'm going to grow here myself."*

(CHAPTER 21)

Before the garden—before Mary and Dickon and the animals, before spring flowers and fresh moor winds, before the joy of having something to look forward to—Colin knew nothing about how beautiful life could be. He only knew about beds and lumps on backs, sick chambers and medication. When Colin finally sees the secret garden for himself and watches spring exploding all around him in riotous color, he is overcome. As he looks at all the growing, blooming things, he realizes that it's a place where he can thrive and grow.

There is something special about the secret garden that speaks to Colin's heart. It's not a trimmed-back "gardener's garden." It's not "all clipped an' spick an' span." Instead, it's been allowed to grow into a glorious profusion of color and variety and wildness. There are no perfect rows of flowers or uniform clipped bushes. From the first, Mary said, "Don't let us make it tidy. . . . It wouldn't seem like a secret garden if it was tidy" (Chapter 11). And Dickon agreed, saying it's better with "things runnin' wild, an' swingin' an' catchin' hold of each other."

The natural tangle of plants, flowers, bushes, and trees is exactly what makes the secret garden so enchanting. Inside, everything buzzes and pulses with life. There is an abundance of things to see and observe and do. Everywhere Colin looks, there are "wonders springing out of the earth or trailing down from trees" (Chapter 21). Every path, nook, and corner brims with life and color. Once Colin is inside the garden, he's mesmerized by it. He wants to watch the secret garden grow—and he wants to grow with it.

The secret garden in full bloom provides a picture of the thriving Christian community God desires for each of us—a place where we can flourish and grow. The body of Christ isn't trimmed and perfect; it's full of variety and giftings and imperfections. It's a place where weakness and growth coexist, burdens are shared, and hearts are tended. Where fellow believers live and work side by side, "swingin' an' catchin' hold of each other," in good times and in bad. And where the family of God builds one another up and invites others in.

In Acts 2, the new believers passionately "devoted themselves to the apostles' teaching and the fellowship, to the breaking of bread and the prayers" (Acts 2:42 ESV). They experienced wonderful miracles, shared their possessions, and took care of one another. Every day, they went to the temple, broke bread in their homes, and praised God. And the Lord "added to their number day by day those who were being saved" (Acts 2:47 ESV). The early church flourished and thrived as its members gathered together and lived out their faith side by side.

And let us consider how we may spur one another on toward love and good deeds, not giving up meeting together, as some are in the habit of doing, but encouraging one another—and all the more as you see the Day approaching.

HEBREWS 10:24–25 NIV

PERSONAL APPLICATION:

We all need a place where we can grow and serve and be encouraged. If you haven't found a church where you can say, "I can grow here," don't give up. Keep praying, asking, and seeking the Lord for this vital part of your walk with Him. Ask Him to direct your steps to other believers who are devoted to studying God's Word, who are serious about prayer, and who are committed to investing in authentic Christian community.

Gathering consistently with other believers is essential to our spiritual health and growth. There are some places and circumstances—and even certain people—that can stunt our spiritual growth or cause us to grow apathetic or stagnant. Other environments stir our faith, inspire our minds, and quicken our hearts. Ask the Lord to make you aware of the places that help you grow and to show you where you can spend your time most wisely.

PRAYER FOR TODAY:

Lord God, thank You for filling the Church with variety and color. I long to be part of a thriving Christian community. Please lead me to the specific places where I can flourish in my faith. Show me the circles and gatherings where I can grow alongside other Christians and join in with making disciples. I want to put down deep roots and use the gifts You've given me so that the whole body of Christ is built up, equipped, and strengthened. Please help me get out of my comfort zone and try new things in these areas of life and ministry: [your prayer]. In Jesus' name, amen.

Let your roots grow down into him, and let your lives be built on him. Then your faith will grow strong in the truth you were taught, and you will overflow with thankfulness.

COLOSSIANS 2:7 NLT

DAY 22
Bold Steps

"If you have faith like a grain of mustard seed, you will say to this mountain, 'Move from here to there,' and it will move, and nothing will be impossible for you."

MATTHEW 17:20 ESV

"I told thee tha' could as soon as tha' stopped bein' afraid," answered Dickon. "An' tha's stopped."
(CHAPTER 22)

This chapter explores the possibilities of what can happen when we let go of fear and take courageous, bold steps forward. When Colin finds out that Ben Weatherstaff—and most other local people—think he can't walk, Colin bravely decides to get up out of his chair and stand up. As everyone watches with delight, Ben exclaims tearfully, "God bless thee!" Dickon says he knew Colin could do it if he "stopped bein' afraid," and Colin responds, "Yes, I've stopped."

But Colin isn't the only one who did something no one else thought was possible. Ben Weatherstaff himself confesses that he has come into the secret garden over the years to prune the roses. The children can't believe it, since the key was buried and lost and "there was no door!" Ben's surprising response: "I didn't come through th' door. I come over th' wall." In answer to the children's questions, Ben explains that Colin's mother had once asked him to always take care of her roses, so to his way of thinking,

"She'd gave her order first."

After walking to a nearby tree, Colin isn't done doing brave new things. Walking leads to digging, and digging leads to planting. As they talk with Ben, Colin picks up Mary's trowel and starts to dig in the soil. The crowning moment is when Ben asks Colin if he'd like to "plant a bit o' somethin'." Colin is delighted by the idea and wants to do so before the sun sets. Everyone bustles around to help him plant a rosebush, creating the perfect ending to a "strange lovely afternoon." As the sun goes down, Colin joyfully stands on his own two feet—"laughing."

When we challenge our fears and take bold steps forward, a whole world of possibilities opens up. When we stop "bein' afraid," we can stand up, walk freely, and start "diggin'" and "plantin'" in God's kingdom. And here's some good news: You don't have to be naturally courageous to take brave steps forward, and you don't have to be physically tough to conquer your fears. You just need the antidote to fear—faith. The even better news is this: Jesus said that faith the size of a tiny mustard seed is enough to move mountains (Matthew 17:20)!

Gideon was not a naturally courageous man. When God called him to lead the Israelites into battle against the Midianites, Gideon listed out all his weaknesses (Judges 6). When God assured Gideon that He would go with him, Gideon asked for a sign. When God graciously gave him one and invited him to make a sacrifice, Gideon was so nervous that he offered it at night so no one would see! After all that, Gideon still asked for two more confirmations—one with wet fleece on dry ground, and another with dry fleece on wet ground—just to be sure. But here's the best part: Gideon's *tiny* faith in a very *big* God eventually helped him overcome his fears and lead the Israelites to victory!

When I am afraid, I put my trust in you.
PSALM 56:3 ESV

PERSONAL APPLICATION:

What's holding you back from taking a brave step forward? What fears do you want to set at God's feet today? Fear comes in many shapes and sizes, but Jesus can help you increase your faith. Whatever it is that seems too big or too scary, ask God to strengthen your wobbly faith and help you stand up and take the next step forward.

What's the courageous thing God has been tapping on your heart to do? It could be the start of something new, an area for spiritual growth, or even a step back from certain responsibilities. It takes bravery to say yes to a new venture, but it also takes courage to say no to something in order to open up your heart and schedule to something the Lord might want you to do. Feeling paralyzed? Start with prayer and focus on taking one step forward this week. Remember: your tiny seed of faith can move mountains.

PRAYER FOR TODAY:

Lord God, I believe that nothing is impossible for You. Thank You that I can trust You with my every need. I want to take new steps of faith and actively trust You more. I confess that my fears and doubts and past experiences often get in the way. Please stir my faith and build my courage. In the places where I've stalled out and I'm sitting still, I want to stand up, walk forward, and start planting new seeds. I especially ask You to help me overcome my unbelief in this area of my life: [your prayer]. In Jesus' name, amen.

———◦◦———

"I do believe; help me overcome my unbelief!"

MARK 9:24 NIV

DAY 23
Faith Unfurls

*The heavens declare the glory
of God, and the sky above
proclaims his handiwork.*

PSALM 19:1 ESV

"Even if it isn't real Magic," Colin said, *"we can pretend it is. Something is there—something!"*
(CHAPTER 23)

In this chapter, Colin becomes uniquely aware that there is "something" in the world—which he calls "Magic"—that makes things blossom and grow. Mary says, "It's Magic. . . but not black. It's as white as snow." And in the "radiant months—the amazing ones" that follow, they see that invisible "something" at work in the garden: green things push "their way through the earth, in the grass, in the beds, even in the crevices of the walls," and buds begin to "unfurl and show color, every shade of blue, every shade of purple, every tint and hue of crimson."

As Colin watches the secret garden grow, he thinks that the Magic can help him grow stronger too. He begins a new health "experiment," which includes an exercise program, hearty meals, positive thinking, and plenty of fresh air each day. He thinks of the Magic as something that is "in everything, only we have not sense enough to get hold of it and make it do things for us—like electricity and horses and steam."

Colin says, "I don't know its name so I call it Magic." He

believes it's what makes the sun rise: "Something pushes it up and draws it." He describes a "feeling of being happy as if something were pushing and drawing in my chest and making me breathe fast." To him, it seems like it is "always pushing and drawing and making things out of nothing." To his thinking, if everything "is made out of Magic," it must be "all around us."

Colin senses that there is an invisible power at work in the world around him, in nature, and in the plants in the garden, and it's true. But the Bible tells us it's not a some-*thing*; it's a some*one*—and His name is Jesus. All creation points to God's very existence and power all around us: "For since the creation of the world God's invisible qualities—his eternal power and divine nature—have been clearly seen, being understood from what has been made, so that people are without excuse" (Romans 1:20 NIV).

In Acts 17:22–28 (NLT), Paul discovered that the people of Athens, who worshipped many gods, had inscribed these words on one of their altars: "To an Unknown God" (v. 23). They were seeking God but didn't know who He was! Seeing an opportunity, Paul proclaimed to them, "This God, whom you worship without knowing, is the one I'm telling you about" (v. 23). He told them that God "made the world and everything in it" and is the "Lord of heaven and earth" (v. 24). He explained that it is God's plan that all people would "seek after God and perhaps feel their way toward him and find him—though he is not far from any one of us" (v. 27).

And the Word became flesh and dwelt among us, and we have seen his glory, glory as of the only Son from the Father, full of grace and truth.

JOHN 1:14 ESV

PERSONAL APPLICATION:

There *is* One who makes the sun rise, causes the plants to bloom, and brings joy to our hearts. God hasn't made Himself hard to find; in fact, He's made Himself evident throughout creation and by revealing Himself to us through the Bible, the prophets, and the testimonies of His people. "You were shown these things so that you might know that the LORD, He is God; there is no other besides Him" (Deuteronomy 4:35 NASB).

If you know someone like Colin who is seeking after "something," pray for an opportunity to tell that person about Jesus. In every seeking heart there is a desire to experience the presence of God and know Him personally. Like Paul, you have been given the privilege to tell your seeking friends, coworkers, and family members who God is.

PRAYER FOR TODAY:

Lord God, thank You for revealing Yourself in creation and in everything around us. I want to study my Bible and learn to share my faith more clearly and fully. Holy Spirit, please lead and guide my steps, give me the words to speak, and empower me to tell others about Jesus. Open my eyes and set up divine appointments with people who are curious about You. I especially pray for the people I love who are seeking "something" but don't yet know You personally: [specific names]. In Jesus' name, amen.

"You will seek me and find me,
when you seek me with all your heart."
JEREMIAH 29:13 ESV

DAY 24
Nourished and Flourishing

Planted in the house of the Lord,
they will flourish in the
courtyards of our God.

PSALM 92:13 NASB

"They're just like th' 'creatures.' If they're thirsty give 'em drink and if they're hungry give 'em a bit o' food."

(CHAPTER 24)

Colin dreams of secretly growing healthy without anyone at Misselthwaite knowing, so he can surprise his father when he comes home. However, he and Mary have a problem: they can't figure out how to get enough good food to eat without tipping off the staff that Colin's health is improving! At breakfast one morning, they bemoan the small servings of ham and muffins. Mary says, "It's enough for a person who is going to die. . .but it's not enough for a person who is going to live." The solution to their problem comes one evening as Dickon works in his cottage garden and talks with his mother in the twilight.

As Mrs. Sowerby sits on the pretty stone wall where Dickon has "tucked moorland foxglove and ferns and rockcress and hedgerow flowers into every crevice," chuckling over their predicament, she has an idea: "When tha' goes to 'em in th' mornin's tha' shall take a pail o' good new milk an' I'll bake 'em a crusty cottage loaf or some buns wi' currants in 'em, same as you children like." The next day, Dickon brings two tin pails with him to the garden: one "full of rich new milk with cream on the top of it" and another with "cottage-made currant buns folded in a clean blue and white napkin, buns so carefully tucked in that they [are] still hot."

Overwhelmed by the delicious "cottage-made" food, Mary and Colin send their shillings to help buy more, and a new tradition of daily feasts begins. Dickon even builds "a sort of tiny oven with stones" in a deep little hollow in the woods: "Roasted eggs were a previously unknown luxury and very hot potatoes with salt and fresh butter in them were fit for a woodland king—besides being deliciously satisfying." Both children grow stronger and healthier each day, being filled to "the brim with roasted eggs and potatoes and richly frothed new milk and oatcakes and buns and heather honey and clotted cream"—delighting all the while in their wonderful secret.

In our spiritual lives, we're "just like th' 'creatures'" too: when we're thirsty, we need a refreshing drink; when we're hungry, we need nourishing food. But many Christians live in a semi-drought and starvation state. We snack on Bible tidbits while stuffing ourselves with too much of what the world has to offer. Instead of getting built up, we end up stressed out. Instead of getting refreshed and energized, we get increasingly tired, anxious, and over-whelmed. Instead of thriving and flourishing, we keep just ahead of drying out.

If we want to experience the abundant life that Jesus promised (John 10:10), we need to eat and drink of God's Word on a consistent basis. First Peter 2:2 (NLT) says, "Like newborn babies, you must crave pure spiritual milk so that you will grow into a full experience of salvation." Hebrews 5:14 (NIV) tells us that "solid food is for the mature," for spiritual training and discernment. We're to live our lives in step with Christ, "rooted and built up in him" and "strengthened in the faith" (Colossians 2:6–7 NIV). Finally, we must "move beyond the elementary teachings about Christ and be taken forward to maturity" (Hebrews 6:1 NIV).

"Do not labor for the food which perishes,
but for the food which endures to everlasting
life, which the Son of Man will give you."
JOHN 6:27 NKJV

PERSONAL APPLICATION:

Mary says one muffin is "enough for a person who is going to die. . .but it's not enough for a person who is going to live." Have you been feeding your soul the right kind of spiritual food? Is your life defined by a consistent, passionate pursuit of joyfully loving and serving Jesus, or do you feel parched or undernourished? If you're hungry for more, it's time to up your intake of healthy spiritual nourishment!

Our souls thrive in certain conditions and wilt in others.

Take a few minutes to evaluate what you read, listen to, and do each week. What are you feeding your mind and spirit? If you see a lot of "junk food" on the list, try substituting those items with something more profitable. Focus on finding spiritual disciplines and activities that stir up your love for Jesus, grow your desire to serve others, and keep you well fed.

PRAYER FOR TODAY:

Thank You, Jesus, for inviting me to experience abundant life in You and thrive in my faith. Sometimes I feel worn down, dried out, and apathetic—like I'm just limping along. I come to You now, the Giver of life, asking for spiritual refilling. Please feed and water my soul. Refresh my spirit with the water of Your Word. Stir my heart with the encouragement and testimony of other believers. Decrease my appetite for the following activities and influences that tend to hinder my growth: [your prayer]. In Jesus' name, amen.

"I came that they may have life and have it abundantly."

JOHN 10:10 ESV

DAY 25
Better Together

*For the body is not
one member, but many.*

1 CORINTHIANS 12:14 KJV

"A hundred rooms no one goes into," [Colin]
said. "It sounds almost like a secret garden.
Suppose we go and look at them."
(CHAPTER 25)

This chapter begins in the "close-grown corner" of the garden where the robin and his mate watch over their precious "Eggs" and watch the children play in the garden. The picture of togetherness—of building something together—extends to the children's lives too. Mary loved the secret garden when it was all her own, but it became much more enjoyable once Dickon joined her and began to help tend, prune, and plant. It became even nicer when they shared it with Colin. They all have more fun in the garden together than if they were on their own.

Even on rainy days when they can't go out to the garden, "it [can] not be said that Mary and Colin [are] dull." Instead of rambling around the house alone when the weather keeps her indoors, Mary now has a companion and friend. Instead of sitting by himself in bed, Colin now has someone to spend time with and new things to think about. But on one rainy day after they've found the garden,

Colin feels as though he'll burst out of his skin if they sit around all day. He has so much energy he can't keep still: "I feel as if I must jump out of bed and shout."

Mary suggests that they explore the house together—and rainy days lose "their terrors that morning." They spend the morning running and exercising, investigating the quiet, rambling rooms and corridors, and playing with the ivory elephants in the cabinet. Together, they see even more rooms and make "more discoveries than Mary had made on her first pilgrimage." They find "new corridors and corners and flights of steps and new old pictures." Both children, who used to be lonely and sickly, unhappy and forlorn, now have a playmate and friend.

So many things are better when we're together, especially during the "rainy days" of life. God created us for fellowship, companionship, and partnership. The theme of togetherness goes back to Genesis, when God made Adam and Eve and when God told Noah to load the animals two by two on the ark (Genesis 7:9). Ecclesiastes 4:9–12 gives an account of the many reasons "two are better than one." And in the New Testament, Jesus underscored the importance of partnership when He sent out His disciples by twos into the countryside to share the Good News (Luke 10:1).

In Exodus 17:8–13 (NKJV), when the Amalekites came against Israel, Moses told Joshua, "Tomorrow I will stand on the top of the hill with the rod of God in my hand" (v. 9). The next day during the battle, whenever Moses held up his hands, "Israel prevailed," but whenever he let his hands drop, "Amalek prevailed" (v. 11). When Moses grew too tired to stand up or hold up his hands any longer, he sat down on a stone. Aaron and Hur "supported his hands, one on one side, and the other on the other side; and his hands were steady until the going down of the sun" (v. 12). The Israelites won the battle that day—because they fought together.

> *Two are better than one, because they*
> *have a good reward for their toil.*
> ECCLESIASTES 4:9 ESV

PERSONAL APPLICATION:

Whether you're in twos or threes or in a larger group, when you join with others to pray, study the Bible, help in your church or community, serve a meal, complete a project, or share the Gospel, everyone benefits from the knowledge, insight, and wisdom that is shared. In the hard times, we shoulder each other's burdens and link arms. Best of all, we get to enjoy the camaraderie that comes from working hard and playing hard together.

Do you ever feel lonely? Are you carrying a heavy burden? Rainy days "lost their terrors" for Mary and Colin when they learned how to make the best of a stormy day— together. When we lift up one another's arms through the battles of this life, we gain the victory together. If you're feeling isolated or you sense the need for others to stand with you in battle, consider joining a community group, signing up to volunteer at your church, or attending a prayer meeting. Rainy days don't have to be lonely days in the family of God.

PRAYER FOR TODAY:

Dear Jesus, thank You for this sweet picture of two children running and exploring and making the best of a rainy day. Open my eyes to what's right in front of me and show me how I can partner with others in this life of faith. Thank You for the godly friends You've brought into my life. Give me the courage to invite more people into my everyday life in an authentic way. Help me to come alongside and hold up the arms of these brothers and sisters in Christ who are burdened with heavy loads: [specific names]. In Jesus' name, amen.

"For where two or three are gathered in my name, there am I among them."

MATTHEW 18:20 ESV

ＯAY 26
From Whom All
Blessings Flow

Come, let us sing to the LORD!
Let us shout joyfully to the
Rock of our salvation.

PSALM 95:1 NLT

*"I'm well! I'm well! I feel—I feel as
if I want to shout out something—
something thankful, joyful!"*
(CHAPTER 26)

When Colin has the sudden realization that he's grown wonderfully healthy and strong, he's overcome by "a sort of rapturous belief and realization" and feels like shouting "something thankful, joyful." Ben Weatherstaff suggests he sing "th' Doxology." Dickon has heard the Doxology sung in church and says his mother believes the "skylarks sings it when they gets up i' th' mornin'." After teaching Colin to stand and take off his cap, Dickon stands "among the trees and rose-bushes" and sings in "quite a simple matter-of-fact way," in a "nice strong boy voice":

Praise God from whom all blessings flow,
Praise Him all creatures here below,
Praise Him above ye Heavenly Host,
Praise Father, Son, and Holy Ghost. Amen.

When Colin asks Dickon to sing it again, he and Mary lift "their voices as musically" as they can, and Dickon's

voice swells "loud and beautiful." Even old Ben clears his
throat and sings "with such vigor that it seem[s] almost
savage." At the "Amen," Ben's chin is "twitching" and he
is "staring and winking and his leathery old cheeks [are]
wet." He declares hoarsely, "I never seed no sense in th'
Doxology afore. . .but I may change my mind i' time."

Just then, Mrs. Sowerby comes quietly into the secret
garden. As they welcome her and show her around, Colin
and Mary look up at her "comfortable rosy face, secretly
curious about the delightful feeling" she gives them—"a
sort of warm, supported feeling." She admires the garden,
speaks tenderly with each of them, and "at the hungry
hour" brings forth a basket packed with "a regular feast."
She is "full of fun" and makes "them laugh at all sorts of
odd things." And when they ask her about the Magic, she
tells them she knows it as "th' Big Good Thing" and "th'
Joy Maker."

There are many people who, like Ben Weatherstaff,
haven't ever "seed no sense" in singing to God, but in time,
they too may change their minds. Others, like Mary and
Colin, don't know what—or whom—to thank when they
feel joyful, but they may be open to learning. And some,
like Susan Sowerby, simply know God as the big, good
"Joy Maker." But wherever our friends, family members,
and coworkers fit on the spectrum of faith, we have the
opportunity to let them know who God is, teach them how
to worship Him—and tell them His name!

Throughout scripture, God revealed Himself and His

name to mankind. In Exodus 3:14 (NASB), God told Moses, "This is what you shall say to the sons of Israel: 'I AM has sent me to you.'" When Isaiah prophesied about the birth of Christ, he said, "His name shall be called Wonderful Counselor, Mighty God, Everlasting Father, Prince of Peace" (Isaiah 9:6 ESV). And when John the Baptist saw Jesus coming toward him to be baptized, he said, "Behold, the Lamb of God, who takes away the sin of the world!" (John 1:29 ESV). All the names of God in the Bible provide a further description of His character, that we might know Him more fully.

> *"And there is salvation in no one else, for*
> *there is no other name under heaven given*
> *among men by which we must be saved."*
> ACTS 4:12 ESV

PERSONAL APPLICATION:

As Christians, we not only get to tell people Jesus' name but also get to tell them about the One from whom *all* blessings flow! In Psalm 96:1–3 (NLT), we are given these wonderful instructions: "Sing a new song to the LORD! Let the whole earth sing to the LORD! Sing to the LORD; praise his name. Each day proclaim the good news that he saves. Publish his glorious deeds among the nations. Tell everyone about the amazing things he does."

This week, take time to read Psalm 96 out loud and practice singing the Doxology with great joy. You don't have to have a beautiful voice to worship the Lord in song! You can praise His name and proclaim to others the Good News that He saves. Go ahead and "publish his glorious deeds" to others, starting with the people you see each day. Tell everyone about the amazing things He has done in your life—things that no one else could do.

PRAYER FOR TODAY:

Dear God, You are the One from whom every good gift and blessing in my life flows. Teach me to lift my voice in praise and adoration, singing to You and glorifying Your name. I want to proclaim Your works and publish Your glorious deeds to the world around me. Show me how to do that in my everyday life. Help me use my gifts in creative ways to declare the Good News. In this area of my life where it's particularly hard to find reasons to be thankful, I pray for Your grace to abound: [your prayer]. In Jesus' name, amen.

Every good and perfect gift is from above, coming down from the Father of the heavenly lights, who does not change like shifting shadows.

JAMES 1:17 NIV

DAY 27
Homecoming

*"Turn to me and be saved, all
the ends of the earth! For I am
God, and there is no other."*

ISAIAH 45:22 ESV

He felt as if he were being drawn back to the place he had so long forsaken, and he did not know why.

(CHAPTER 27)

In this final chapter of *The Secret Garden*, we discover that while "the secret garden was coming alive and two children were coming alive with it," Mr. Craven has wandered far from home. In an effort to outrun his pain, he's visited many "far-away beautiful places." He's "kept his mind filled with dark and heart-broken thinking," allowed his soul to "fill itself with blackness," and refused "obstinately to allow any rift of light to pierce through." In his wandering, he's "forgotten and deserted his home and his duties."

But on the very day when Colin stands in the secret garden and cries, "I'm going to live forever!" something "strange" happens to Mr. Craven. As he sits by a stream in a beautiful valley, his troubled "mind and body both grow quiet, as quiet as the valley itself." He feels a change within and whispers, "I almost feel as if—I were alive!" Over the next few days, his soul awakens, he starts to wonder about Colin, and he dreams his wife is calling for him "in the garden." When a letter arrives from Mrs. Sowerby, he knows it's time to go home.

When Mr. Craven stops running from his pain and turns his feet homeward, everything changes. He begins to think, "Perhaps I have been all wrong for ten years." At home, he feels as though he's being "drawn back to the place he had so long forsaken." And finally, when he meets his tall, handsome, healthy son, he finds the healing he's needed since his wife died. He asks Colin to take him into the garden and tell him "all about it." There, all their secrets become secrets no more—and father and son walk back to the house together, united at last.

Just as Mr. Craven must stop running away and turn toward home in order to find wholeness again, so there must be a turning toward God in each of our lives. There is a onetime turning that we all must choose, when we turn from our sin and put our trust in Jesus for our salvation. But also, anytime we encounter brokenness, grief, pain, or sin, we need to continually turn toward God. Running away only prolongs the pain and delays the healing process. When we bring all our troubles to Him, our secrets become secrets no more—and we are set free!

In the parable of the prodigal son in Luke 15:11–32 (ESV), the son took his inheritance and ran away from home to live a life of pleasure. He enjoyed himself to the fullest, but eventually his sin and his choices caught up with him. Ruined and out of money, he finally came to his senses. He began to consider his home and his father—and his sin.

He turned his feet toward home, went back, and repented: "Father, I have sinned against heaven and before you. I am no longer worthy to be called your son" (v. 21). And his father, a picture of our heavenly Father, forgave him and welcomed him with open arms.

> *"For this my son was dead, and is alive*
> *again; he was lost, and is found."*
> LUKE 15:24 ESV

PERSONAL APPLICATION:

We were all prodigals at one time—and sometimes, even in our daily stubbornness, we continue to walk on our own paths. We run from God's correction, from painful situations, from the process of grieving, and even from God's calling on our lives. In every case, a turning is required. When you turn to Jesus, surrendering everything to Him, you *will* find peace. Everything is better when you walk hand in hand with your heavenly Father.

Do you know friends or family members who are running away from God or wandering far from home? Don't give up praying for them. Pray that they would stop walking away and stand still. Pray that the Lord would awaken their hearts and flood their lives with His light. Pray for God to surround them with other Christians who can share the Gospel in a way that draws them to Jesus. And pray for

God to turn their hearts—and feet—homeward.

PRAYER FOR TODAY:

Lord God, I give You my life and my feet that are so prone to wander. Help me to stay on Your paths and walk in Your ways. May the words of my mouth and the meditation of my heart be pleasing to You (Psalm 19:14). I pray now for those whom I love who are wandering far from home and from You right now, Lord. Please have mercy on each one and gently call them home. I lift up to You this area of my own life where I have been running away and need to turn back to You: [your prayer]. In Jesus' name, amen.

Therefore repent and return, so that your sins may be wiped away, in order that times of refreshing may come from the presence of the Lord.

ACTS 3:19 NASB

ᗡAY 28
Hearts like Flowers

*Keep your heart with all vigilance,
for from it flow the springs of life.*

PROVERBS 4:23 ESV

Mistress Mary always felt that however many years she lived she should never forget that first morning when her garden began to grow.

(CHAPTER 11)

At the close of *The Secret Garden*, there is an overarching lesson for us to remember and take away with us: gardens require tending. We first see this theme when Mary discovers the secret garden. Although there are signs of life, it's been neglected. Some of it has died, while other parts have run wild. She has no idea if anything will bloom, but she begins to dig around the little green spikes poking up through the grass because she instinctively knows that they will have a better chance of thriving if they have space to breathe and grow.

Next, Ben Weatherstaff's work in the kitchen gardens reminds us that caring for a garden is a year-round job. Even in the dead of winter, when things look "bare and ugly," Ben works. He doesn't stop and put up his feet; he digs and prepares the soil during the coldest months, looking forward to what's to come. Though he has little to show for his labor for months at a time, he keeps on with it because he knows from experience the truth about gardening: if you tend the soil during the winter, plants will start "stirrin' down below in th' dark" come spring.

Finally, Dickon's work in his cottage garden teaches us that small, consistent investments reap a bountiful harvest. He works early in the morning and late in the "fading twilight" every day. He digs and weeds and plants wisely, purchasing "seeds he could save year after year" and plants "whose roots would bloom each spring and spread in time into fine clumps." And all along, he tucks "moorland foxglove and ferns and rock-cress and hedgerow flowers" into every crevice of the stone wall. The result: plentiful vegetables and herbs throughout the year.

Hearts, like gardens, also require tending. Proverbs 4:23 (esv) says, "Keep your heart with all vigilance, for from it flow the springs of life." Thus, just like a wise gardener, we must continually tend to our hearts in order to see a fruitful spiritual harvest. There is pruning back, storing up, and planting that's needed; digging, rooting, and planning to do; tender green shoots of life to nurture; and blossom and bounty to share. Best of all, in every season, God has kingdom work for us to do and people for us to meet and encourage along the way.

When Paul went to Philippi (Acts 16:13–15), he looked for the best place to share the Good News about Jesus. When he heard about a prayer meeting by the river outside the city on the Sabbath, he went. He met a group of women there who had gathered to pray, including Lydia, a worshipper of God. As Paul taught about Jesus, God opened her heart and she responded. Lydia and her entire household were baptized that day, and a church later formed in her house—all because Paul took the time to care for the spiritual needs of a group of praying women!

Preach the word; be prepared in season and out of season; correct, rebuke and encourage— with great patience and careful instruction.

2 Timothy 4:2 niv

PERSONAL APPLICATION:

Are you taking good care of your own heart? Be sure to give your soul room to grow and your spirit fresh air to breathe. Make consistent daily investments in your relationship with God in order to see long-term benefits. And remember this: when you persevere in even the most dry and barren seasons, you *will* reap dividends later down the road.

Where do you see signs of life around you? Are there other hearts God may be asking you to help tend? Ask Him to show you where you can begin to dig and plant seeds of faith. Look for people who are open to the Gospel. Keep your eyes open for those who are longing for community. Talk with people who are asking questions about God. Help your friends understand God's love for them and His glorious purpose for their lives.

PRAYER FOR TODAY:

Lord, thank You for tending to my heart in every season. Lead me as I draw close to You through my daily devotions. Show me where I need to take better care of my spirit and where I might be ignoring signs of dryness or letting weeds grow. Make me like a well-watered garden in Your sight. Help me recognize the people around me who desire to know You more, and show me how to share my faith naturally. Please encourage my heart, especially in the places that have been neglected and need more space to breathe and grow: [your prayer]. In Jesus' name, amen.

———————◆◆◆———————

"You will be like a well-watered garden,
like a spring whose waters never fail."
ISAIAH 58:11 NIV

DAY 29
A Fruitful Bough

"May God Almighty bless you and make you fruitful and increase your numbers until you become a community of peoples."

GENESIS 28:3 NIV

*And the secret garden bloomed and bloomed
and every morning revealed new miracles.*
(CHAPTER 25)

In the secret garden, the seeds and bulbs send out shoots and the climbing rosebushes spread and grow until the whole garden is covered in "a green mist" that's "almost like a green gauze veil" in early spring. Soon after, bright spots of color begin to burst from every crack and crevice. By summer, the garden blooms and blooms, revealing "new miracles" every morning. Come fall, the garden has undergone a complete change:

> *The place was a wilderness of autumn gold and purple and violet blue and flaming scarlet and on every side were sheaves of late lilies standing together—lilies which were white or white and ruby. . . . Late roses climbed and hung and clustered and the sunshine deepening the hue of the yellowing trees made one feel that one, stood in an embowered temple of gold.*

In Mary's life, a similar transformation takes place. Though her own fractured family tree is full of broken branches and wilted leaves, she discovers that Misselthwaite isn't all dead. She meets the Sowerby family, with all their homespun goodness, and learns how to live and work and take an interest in the world around her. Through the spring and summer months, she blossoms right along with the garden.

But the fruitful multiplication of life and wholeness doesn't stop there. In the midst of her own renewal, Mary meets her cousin Colin and passes on what she's learning. Then, once the two cousins grow healthier and happier, Colin's thoughts naturally turn to his father. And when Mr. Craven returns home, more healing and restoration comes. The Craven family tree, despite its deep scars, is mended and made whole again—and bursts into full bloom.

As the characters in *The Secret Garden* begin to thrive, they share the bounty with others. In a similar way, when you begin to flourish in your faith, God calls you to then pass on what you've learned and help others blossom as well. As you grow closer to the heart of God, you can multiply that faith to others. In doing so, your life will "bloom and bloom" and "every morning reveal new miracles" of God's grace to the world around you.

The Bible provides many examples of people who multiplied their faith in practical ways. Moses trained Joshua to lead the nation of Israel (Deuteronomy 3:28). Elijah passed along his experience and knowledge of God to Elisha and gave him his mantle (1 Kings 19:19–21). Naomi taught Ruth how to follow God and guided her with wisdom and instruction. Elizabeth confirmed that Mary was carrying the Messiah and encouraged her (Luke 1:41–45). And Paul taught Timothy, Titus, and many others how to spread the Gospel, plant churches, and lead ministries. Fruitful spiritual multiplication is how the kingdom of God grows here on earth.

> *"I chose you and appointed you*
> *that you should go and bear fruit."*
> JOHN 15:16 NKJV

PERSONAL APPLICATION:

The Sowerby family had very little in terms of education or material possessions, but they made a huge impact on the Craven family by simply sharing generously of all they had and knew. Mrs. Sowerby took a motherly interest in Mary and Colin and helped them grow and flourish. Keeping that in mind and considering all God has given you, what can you share with others that can help them grow in their faith?

This is your call to use the gifts, talents, and practical knowledge God has given you! Look for ways to bring others along with you on the journey and pass on what God is teaching you. As you consecrate your life to the Lord,

He will bless the work of your hands and multiply your efforts in ways you can't imagine.

PRAYER FOR TODAY:

Lord God, thank You for all the people who have encouraged me in my faith and shared their lives with me. I want to be fruitful and multiply what You've given me and help people follow You and love You. Help me share with others the joy of knowing You. I offer up my time and my talents, and I ask You to show me where I can serve You best. I especially consecrate to You the following gifts and interests You've given me, that I might steward them well and use them to bring glory to Your name: [your prayer]. In Jesus' name, amen.

"But you will receive power when the Holy Spirit comes on you; and you will be my witnesses in Jerusalem, and in all Judea and Samaria, and to the ends of the earth."

ACTS 1:8 NIV

DAY 30
The Key to the Garden
(A Special Invitation)

"You will seek me and find me,
when you seek me with
all your heart."

JEREMIAH 29:13 ESV

"Perhaps it has been buried for ten years," [Mary] said in a whisper. "Perhaps it is the key to the garden!"
(CHAPTER 7)

Mary first hears about the secret garden from Martha, who tells her it's been "locked up" for "ten years." When she asks why, Martha says, "Mr. Craven had it shut when his wife died so sudden. He won't let no one go inside. It was her garden. He locked th' door an' dug a hole and buried th' key." Mary is instantly curious and can't "help thinking about the garden which no one had been into for ten years" from that moment forward. She longs to find that mysterious, hidden garden—and she doesn't give up until she does.

When Mary later glimpses the robin "swinging on a tree-top" inside the "garden no one can go into," she is determined to find a way in. She walks around the walls of the garden each day, but there appears to be "no door." However, she knows "there must have been [a door] ten years ago" because Mr. Craven locked it and buried the key. As she carefully examines the ivy walls, Mary thinks it's "silly" to be so close to the garden but "not be able to get in" (Chapter 8).

Mary's persistent searching, along with help from the robin, leads her to the key and finally to the door of the garden. When she finds the key, she decides to keep it with her always. When she finally glimpses the handle of the door, she doesn't hesitate for even one moment—"she jump[s] toward it and [catches] it in her hand." And once she's inside, she is overjoyed by the thought that she can now "come through the door under the ivy any time."

In much the same way, the kingdom of God has a key as well—the key of faith. Like the door to the garden, our sin separates us from fellowship with God, but faith in Jesus Christ unlocks the door to eternal life and reconciles us to God. By accepting Christ's blood shed for us, we are cleansed of all unrighteousness and set free from sin and death. We become coheirs with Christ and join the family of God and His glorious kingdom forever.

Jesus truly is "the key" to the Garden of Life: "Salvation is found in no one else, for there is no other name under heaven given to mankind by which we must be saved" (Acts 4:12 NIV). Jesus said, "I am the way, and the truth, and the life. No one comes to the Father except through me" (John 14:6 ESV). The Bible says we have all sinned and fallen short of the glory of God (Romans 3:23), but the Good News is this: Jesus gave His life as a ransom for the sins of the world (Matthew 20:28), that all who believe in Him might have everlasting life (John 3:16).

If you declare with your mouth, "Jesus is Lord," and believe in your heart that God raised him from the dead, you will be saved.

ROMANS 10:9 NIV

———◦•◦———

PERSONAL APPLICATION:

Notice that once Mary found the key to the garden, she was able to go "through the door under the ivy any time." What a glorious symbol of the access we've been given to God's throne of grace through faith in Jesus (Hebrews 4:16). You can go to Him anytime, anywhere—for any reason. The key of faith doesn't open the door to fellowship with God one time; it opens the door for *all* time.

If you've been searching for God and want to know Him personally, God is waiting with open arms to greet you! "You will seek me and find me, when you seek me with all your heart" (Jeremiah 29:13 ESV). If you want to come "into the garden" of faith and walk with God, you can do that today. The door to knowing God is not closed, no matter who you are, what you've done, or where you're from. All you need is the key of faith.

PRAYER FOR TODAY:

Lord God, I come before You today with open hands and a thankful heart. Thank You for making known to me the key of faith and the path of eternal life. Thank You for revealing Yourself to me and for calling me into a personal relationship with You. I love walking closely with You every day. Thank You for granting me continual access to Your throne of grace, Lord. Please help me to more persistently seek You in my everyday decisions and in this specific situation: [your prayer]. In Jesus' name, amen.

PRAYER FOR SALVATION:

Dear Jesus, please come into my heart and forgive me of all my sins. Wash me clean and make me new. I ask You to be my Lord and Savior, that I might become a child of God. I give You my life and all that I have. I want to walk with You and talk with You every day. Thank You for saving me. Thank You for the gift of eternal life. I'm so glad to be Yours forever. In Jesus' name, amen.

But to all who did receive him, who believed in his name, he gave the right to become children of God.

JOHN 1:12 ESV

Author's Note

As you come to the close of this devotional book, it's my prayer that you've been refreshed and revived in your personal walk with God. I hope that you will take with you all the reminders and promises you've read so that you can flourish in your faith no matter what life brings or what season you find yourself in.

If you've been encouraged by this book, please consider sharing it with your friends and family members who may be walking through a dry or wintry season. You might even offer to read it together, alongside *The Secret Garden*, so that you can build one another up, pray together, and share your burdens with each other.

If you prayed to receive Jesus as your personal Savior, or if you want to know more about the Bible or how to grow in your walk with God, I'd love to hear from you and help you take the next step in your faith! You can connect with me online at RachelDodge.com to send me a message or write to me via my social media accounts.

Like roses in a garden, we are called to spread out and send forth beautiful shoots of faith in this world as we glorify God and help others know Him. May your life be like a flourishing garden, consecrated to God and pleasing in His sight.

May the Lord bless you and keep you always!

Blossom and Bloom: Flowers and Plants of *The Secret Garden*

Have you ever wished you could have your very own secret garden? Though most of us do not have access to a walled garden in Yorkshire, you can still tend a "bit of earth" that's all your own and watch it come alive! All you need is a flower bed in your yard, a few pots on your patio or deck, or a selection of small containers in your windowsill.

The following is a collection of quotes detailing many of the flowers and plants mentioned in *The Secret Garden*. If you've ever wanted to create a pretty nook that's all your own, may these descriptions provide the inspiration you need to get started!

"Just you wait till you see th' gold-colored gorse blossoms an' th' blossoms o' th' broom, an' th' heather flowerin', all purple bells, an' hundreds o' butterflies flutterin' an' bees hummin' an' skylarks soarin' up an' singin'." (ch. 7)

It was the sweetest, most mysterious-looking place anyone could imagine. (ch. 9)

The high walls which shut it in were covered with the leafless stems of climbing roses which were so thick that they were matted together. (ch. 9)

All the ground was covered with grass of a wintry brown and out of it grew clumps of bushes which were surely rosebushes if they were alive. There were numbers of standard roses which had so spread their branches that they were like little trees. (ch. 9)

There were other trees in the garden, and one of the things which made the place look strangest and loveliest was that climbing roses had run all over them and swung down long tendrils which made light swaying curtains, and here and there they had caught at each other or at a far-reaching branch and had crept from one tree to another and made lovely bridges of themselves. (ch. 9)

There seemed to have been grass paths here and there, and in one or two corners there were alcoves of evergreen with stone seats or tall moss-covered flower urns in them. (ch. 9)

"Martha," [Mary] said, "what are those white roots that look like onions?"

"They're bulbs," answered Martha. "Lots o' spring flowers grow from 'em. Th' very little ones are snowdrops an' crocuses an' th' big ones are narcissuses an' jonquils and daffydowndillys. Th' biggest of all is lilies an' purple flags. Eh! they are nice. Dickon's got a whole lot of 'em planted in our bit o' garden." (ch. 9)

"There's a place in th' park woods here where there's snowdrops by thousands. They're the prettiest sight in Yorkshire when th' spring comes. No one knows when they was first planted." (ch. 9)

The bulbs in the secret garden must have been much astonished. Such nice clear places were made round them that they had all the breathing space they wanted, and really, if Mistress Mary had known it, they began to cheer up under the dark earth and work tremendously. The sun could get at them and warm them, and when the rain came down it could reach them at once, so they began to feel very much alive. (ch. 10)

"I've got th' garden tools. There's a little spade an' rake an' a fork an' hoe. Eh! they are good 'uns. There's a trowel, too. An' th' woman in th' shop threw in a packet o' white poppy an' one o' blue larkspur when I bought th' other seeds." (Dickon, ch. 10)

"There's a lot o' mignonette an' poppies," [Dickon] said. "Mignonette's th' sweetest smellin' thing as grows, an' it'll grow wherever you cast it, same as poppies will. Them as'll come up an' bloom if you just whistle to 'em, them's th' nicest of all." (ch. 10)

"They're crocuses an' snowdrops, an' these here is narcissuses," turning to another patch, "an' here's daffydowndillys. Eh! they will be a sight." (Dickon, ch. 11)

"I wouldn't want to make it look like a gardener's garden, all clipped an' spick an' span, would you?" [Dickon] said. "It's nicer like this with things runnin' wild, an' swingin' an' catchin' hold of each other." (ch. 11)

"Don't let us make it tidy," said Mary anxiously. "It wouldn't seem like a secret garden if it was tidy." (ch. 11)

"Are there any flowers that look like bells?" [Mary] inquired. "Lilies o' th' valley does," [Dickon] answered, digging away with the trowel, "an' there's Canterbury bells, an' campanulas."

"Let's plant some," said Mary.

"There's lilies o' th' valley here already; I saw 'em. They'll have growed too close an' we'll have to separate 'em, but there's plenty. Th' other ones takes two years to bloom from seed, but I can bring you some bits o' plants from our cottage garden." (ch. 11)

The long warm rain had done strange things to the herbaceous beds which bordered the walk by the lower wall. There were things sprouting and pushing out from the roots of clumps of plants and there were actually here and there glimpses of royal purple and yellow unfurling among the stems of crocuses. (ch. 15)

Already nearly all the weeds were cleared out of the garden and most of the roses and trees had been pruned or dug about. Dickon had brought a spade of his own and he had taught Mary to use all her tools, so that by this time it was plain that though the lovely wild place was not likely to become a "gardener's garden" it would be a wilderness of growing things before the springtime was over. (ch. 16)

"There'll be apple blossoms an' cherry blossoms overhead," Dickon said, working away with all his might. "An' there'll be peach an' plum trees in bloom against th' walls, an' th' grass'll be a carpet o' flowers." (ch. 16)

"I think it has been left alone so long—that it has grown all into a lovely tangle. I think the roses have climbed and climbed and climbed until they hang from the branches and walls and creep over the ground—almost like a strange gray mist. Some of them have died but many—are alive and when the summer comes there will be curtains and fountains of roses. I think the ground is full of daffodils and snowdrops and lilies and iris working their way out of the dark." (Mary, ch. 17)

"Perhaps they are coming up through the grass—perhaps there are clusters of purple crocuses and gold ones—even now. Perhaps the leaves are beginning to break out and uncurl—and perhaps—the gray is changing and a green gauze veil is creeping—and creeping over—everything. And the birds are coming to look at it—because it is—so safe and still. And perhaps—perhaps—perhaps—" very softly and slowly indeed, "the robin has found a mate—and is building a nest." (Mary, ch. 17)

"Those long spires of blue ones—we'll have a lot of those," Colin was announcing. "They're called Del-phin-iums."

"Dickon says they're larkspurs made big and grand," cried Mistress Mary. "There are clumps there already." (ch. 19)

"Things are crowding up out of the earth," [Mary] ran on in a hurry. "And there are flowers uncurling and buds on everything and the green veil has covered nearly all the gray and the birds are in such a hurry about their nests for fear they may be too late that some of them are even fighting for places in the secret garden. And the rose-bushes look as wick as wick can be, and there are primroses in the lanes and woods, and the seeds we planted are up, and Dickon has brought the fox and the crow and the squirrels and a new-born lamb." (ch. 19)

"I couldna' say that there name," [Dickon] said, pointing to one under which was written "Aquilegia," "but us calls that a columbine, an' that there one it's a snapdragon and they both grow wild in hedges, but these is garden ones an' they're bigger an' grander. There's some big clumps o' columbine in th' garden. They'll look like a bed o' blue an' white butterflies flutterin' when they're out." (ch. 19)

Over walls and earth and trees and swinging sprays and tendrils the fair green veil of tender little leaves had crept, and in the grass under the trees and the gray urns in the alcoves and here and there everywhere were touches or splashes of gold and purple and white and the trees were showing pink and snow above his head and there were fluttering of wings and faint sweet pipes and humming and scents and scents. (ch. 20)

They drew the chair under the plum-tree, which was snow-white with blossoms and musical with bees. It was like a king's canopy, a fairy king's. There were flowering cherry-trees near and apple-trees whose buds were pink and white, and here and there one had burst open wide. Between the blossoming branches of the canopy bits of blue sky looked down like wonderful eyes. (ch. 21)

Dickon had bought penny packages of flower seeds now and then and sown bright sweet-scented things among gooseberry bushes and even cabbages and he grew borders of mignonette and pinks and pansies and things whose seeds he could save year after year or whose roots would bloom each spring and spread in time into fine clumps. The low wall was one of the prettiest things in Yorkshire because he had tucked moorland foxglove and ferns and rock-cress and hedgerow flowers into every crevice until only here and there glimpses of the stones were to be seen. (ch. 24)

The place was a wilderness of autumn gold and purple and violet blue and flaming scarlet and on every side were sheaves of late lilies standing together—lilies which were white or white and ruby. He remembered well when the first of them had been planted that just at this season of the year their late glories should reveal themselves. Late roses climbed and hung and clustered and the sunshine deepening the hue of the yellowing trees made one feel that one, stood in an embowered temple of gold. (ch. 27)

Nourish and Thrive:
Mrs. Sowerby's
"Cottage–Made" Victuals

The descriptions of food in *The Secret Garden* certainly make the mouth water! The following is a collection of quotes detailing the delicious "cottage-made" food that the Sowerby family ate, cooked, and shared with Colin and Mary in the novel. If you feel so inclined, you might pack a hamper on a sunny day and create a Yorkshire picnic for your family or friends!

[Martha] was full of stories of the delights of her day out. Her mother had been glad to see her and they had got the baking and washing all out of the way. She had even made each of the children a doughcake with a bit of brown sugar in it. "I had 'em all pipin' hot when they came in from playin' on th' moor. An' th' cottage all smelt o' nice, clean hot bakin' an' there was a good fire, an' they just shouted for joy." (ch. 8)

"[I will ask] if you might be driven over to our cottage some day and have a bit o' mother's hot oat cake, an' butter, an' a glass o' milk." (ch. 9)

"My dinner's easy to carry about with me," [Dickon] said. "Mother always lets me put a bit o' somethin' in my pocket." He picked up his coat from the grass and brought out of a pocket a lumpy little bundle tied up in a quite clean, coarse, blue and white handkerchief. It held two thick pieces of bread with a slice of something laid between them. "It's oftenest naught but bread," he said, "but I've got a fine slice o' fat bacon with it today." (ch. 11)

"I'll tell thee what, lad," Mrs. Sowerby said when she could speak. "I've thought of a way to help 'em. When tha' goes to 'em in th' mornin's tha' shall take a pail o' good new milk an' I'll bake 'em a crusty cottage loaf or some buns wi' currants in 'em, same as you children like. Nothin's so good as fresh milk an' bread. Then they could take off th' edge o' their hunger while they were in their garden an' th' fine food they get indoors 'ud polish off th' corners." (ch. 24)

The morning that Dickon. . .went behind a big rosebush and brought forth two tin pails and revealed that one was full of rich new milk with cream on the top of it, and that the other held cottage-made currant buns folded in a clean blue and white napkin, buns so carefully tucked in that they were still hot, there was a riot of surprised joyfulness. What a wonderful thing for Mrs. Sowerby to think of! What a kind, clever woman she must be! How good the buns were! And what delicious fresh milk! (ch. 24)

Dickon made the stimulating discovery that in the wood in the park outside the garden where Mary had first found him piping to the wild creatures there was a deep little hollow where you could build a sort of tiny oven with stones and roast potatoes and eggs in it. Roasted eggs were a previously unknown luxury and very hot potatoes with salt and fresh butter in them were fit for a woodland king—besides being deliciously satisfying. (ch. 24)

You can trifle with your breakfast and seem to disdain your dinner if you are full to the brim with roasted eggs and potatoes and richly frothed new milk and oatcakes and buns and heather honey and clotted cream. (ch. 24)

"I couldn't help remembering that last big potato you ate and the way your mouth stretched when you bit through that thick lovely crust with jam and clotted cream on it." (Mary, ch. 24)

[Mrs. Sowerby] had packed a basket which held a regular feast this morning, and when the hungry hour came and Dickon brought it out from its hiding place, she sat down with them under their tree and watched them devour their food, laughing and quite gloating over their appetites. (ch. 26)

Acknowledgments

I'm incredibly grateful for the opportunity to write and publish this book, enjoy the splendor of God's Word each day as I work, and share the love of Jesus through my love of writing and classic literature.

Thank you to the following people for their prayers and support on this journey:

Janet Grant of Books & Such Literary Management for representing me and my writing so that people around the world can find encouragement in their faith through the books God has put on my heart to write.

The entire team at Barbour Publishing who helped make this book possible. Thank you to Annie Tipton for giving me the opportunity to write this book and for her continual support. Thank you to Shalyn Sattler and Abbey Bible for their help with marketing and promotions and all the other "magic" they make behind the scenes.

Jeane Wynn for her help promoting my books and for her friendship and support through the ups and downs of launching books into the world.

My friends and prayer partners: Courtney Boudreau, Nina Ruth Bruno, Carolyn Frank, Tammy Gurzhiy, Katie Kuhl, Sarah Magee, Sarah Matye, Hennie McIntire, Krissy Miller, Shauna Pilgreen, Taylre Nelson, Leona Souza, Jenice Williams, and Kristina Van Coops.

My parents, George and Ruth, for believing in me—always—and for introducing me to great books at an early age. Thank you, Dad, for being my faithful first reader.

My brother, Matthew, for keeping me inspired with deep talks about writing and books.

My children, Lizzy and Jack, for always loving me and supporting me, especially when I'm worn out and need a hug or a laugh. You help keep things bright and happy in our home!

And my husband, Bobby, for his continual support of my writing life and ministry. You always know how to get me up and going again when I start to fade. You make me sleep when I don't want to, and you make me laugh when I think I can't. Thank you for checking all my references and for keeping me sane. I couldn't do this without you!

Finally, thank you to Frances Hodgson Burnett for writing *The Secret Garden* in the first place and for giving readers around the world a reason to believe that no matter how dreary things might seem, spring is just around the corner!

Bibliography

Burnett, Frances Hodgson. *The Secret Garden* (1911). Urbana, Illinois: Project Gutenberg, 2001.

About the Author

Rachel Dodge is a college English instructor and the bestselling author of *The Little Women Devotional: A Chapter-by-Chapter Companion to Louisa May Alcott's Beloved Classic*, the award-winning *Anne of Green Gables Devotional: A Chapter-by-Chapter Companion for Kindred Spirits*, and *Praying with Jane: 31 Days through the Prayers of Jane Austen*. A true kindred spirit at heart, Rachel loves books, bonnets, and ball gowns. When she's not writing, Rachel enjoys spending time with her husband and two children and their fluffy white dog. You can visit her online at RachelDodge.com.

Other Books by Rachel Dodge

The Anne of Green Gables Devotional

This beautiful devotional offers lovely inspiration that explores the theme of God's love and faithfulness through the pages of the classic L. M. Montgomery novel. This collector's volume includes original artwork throughout, and each devotion includes examples from the novel, scripture, life application questions, and prayers.

Hardback / 978-1-64352-616-4

The Little Women Devotional

This devotional explores the themes of faith, family, contentment, widom, and joy in the classic Louisa May Alcott novel. This beautiful chapter-by-chapter devotional includes original artwork throughout, and each reading includes examples from the novel, scripture, life application, and prayers. Turn the page for an extended preview!

Hardback / 978-1-63609-096-2

A Little Women
WELCOME

I'll never forget the first time my mother put a copy of Louisa May Alcott's *Little Women* in my hands. She said, "You will love it, but it will make you cry."

And isn't that true? *Little Women* has warmed hearts for generations now—making us laugh, smile, *and* cry each time we read it. The story is sweet and tender, familiar and comforting. Even the names of the characters—Marmee, Meg, Jo, Beth, Amy, and Laurie—evoke vibrant memories. Opening the first few pages of *Little Women* feels like stepping in the front door of the March home and joining the cozy family circle by the fire.

When we think of the March family, nostalgic images of hearth and home immediately come to mind. We picture a snug house bursting with activity, plays and club meetings up in the garret, hymns around the piano by candlelight, and lively meals at the table. Most of all, we imagine a dear family that loves together, prays together, and believes together.

Though it was written long ago, *Little Women* still strikes a chord with readers today. Its relatable characters and themes stand the test of time. In it we read about family and friends, war and peace, work and calling, love and loss. We learn that hard work is good for us and a cheerful heart makes it more enjoyable. We discover that the key to contentment isn't found in having everything we want but in learning to make much of what we've been given.

Little Women is also a treasure trove of timeless spiritual themes. Many of its lessons and motifs are drawn from the Bible, *Pilgrim's Progress* by John Bunyan, and other Christian writings. In the March home, Christian morals are valued and practiced. Faith, hope, and love abound. Mr. March leads his family with loving care and patient kindness. Mrs. March ("Marmee") teaches and trains her daughters with tenderness and practical wisdom. The March sisters learn to pray, have personal devotions, and walk with God in their daily lives. And faith is at the center of it all.

Finally, *Little Women* shows us what it looks like to live in close community with other believers. In the March family—as in the family of God—everyone has a part to play and no one walks alone. As they work and live side by side, they soften each other's rough edges and sharpen one another as "iron sharpens iron" (Proverbs 27:17). They each use their unique gifts and talents to serve the Lord and others. They learn to care for their neighbors, comfort each other in their afflictions, hold fast to God's Word, walk in close relationship with Jesus, and invite others to gather with them around the fellowship table.

<hr />

You are holding this book in your hands for a reason. The Lord wants to meet with you and speak to you through His Word. As you spend time with Him each day, your faith will grow and flourish. God will direct your path, comfort you, and encourage you. Listen for His voice, and keep a notebook and a pen handy so you can take note of all you're learning. Press into Jesus, and allow Him to do a new work in your heart and life.

In this book, you'll find one devotional entry for every corresponding chapter of *Little Women*, each with key moments from that chapter of the novel, thoughts for personal reflection, selected Bible passages, and a short prayer. When you sit down to read, take time to prepare your heart. Invite the Holy Spirit to speak and move. Come to God with a posture to receive—hands open, head bowed, heart humble.

As you begin this journey, I invite you to curl up in a cozy spot and enjoy a nostalgic visit with the March family. There is so much God wants to do in your life. Things He wants to teach you and show you. Wounds He wants to heal. Places where He is calling you to serve. And a unique role for you to play in His kingdom. May your time reading this devotional inspire a new-found joy in the Lord, a greater passion for Jesus, and a deeper understanding of His plans and purposes for your life.

Day 1

BEGIN AGAIN
IN EARNEST

*Live a life worthy of the Lord and please him
in every way: bearing fruit in every good work,
growing in the knowledge of God.*

COLOSSIANS 1:10 NIV

Little Women opens with Meg, Jo, Beth, and Amy by the fire, "knitting away in the twilight," sighing over a "Christmas without any presents," and lamenting the absence of Father, who is "far away, where the fighting is." They decide to buy gifts for themselves and "have a little fun," but when Beth sets Marmee's slippers on the hearth to warm, the "sight of the old shoes" has a "good effect upon the girls." They decide to spend their money on Marmee instead.

After supper the girls gather close around Marmee's chair to read a letter from Father and the special note he included for his "little girls at home." He says he thinks of them by day and prays for them by night. And he encourages them to use their time apart to "do their duty faithfully, fight their bosom enemies bravely, and conquer themselves so beautifully" that when he comes home, he may be "fonder and prouder than ever of [his] little women."

As the girls sniff back tears, Marmee reminds them of how they used to "play pilgrims" from *Pilgrim's Progress* as little girls. She inspires them to "begin again, not in play, but in earnest,"

217

now that they are older, and see how far they can get in their journey of faith before Father comes home. Delighted with the idea, they agree to try it and start making plans. Marmee tells them to look for their "guidebooks" under their pillows on Christmas morning.

Like the March sisters, we all are on a pilgrimage. As followers of Jesus Christ, this world is not our permanent home (Hebrews 13:14). But while we're here, we've been given important work to do: We each have a road to travel, burdens to carry, and weaknesses to overcome. We have people to love and duties to fulfill. And every day we have the opportunity to "begin again, not in play, but in earnest" on our journey toward loving Jesus more and pleasing Him in every way (Colossians 1:10).

In the New Testament, we find an inspiring picture of what it looks like to follow Jesus "in earnest." After Jesus ascended into heaven, His followers "devoted themselves to the apostles' teaching and the fellowship, to the breaking of bread and the prayers" (Acts 2:42 ESV). Each day, they attended services together at the temple and broke bread in their homes (Acts 2:46). And everywhere they went, they told people about Jesus. As a result, "the Lord added to their number day by day those who were being saved" (Acts 2:47 ESV).

> *Let us also lay aside every weight, and sin*
> *which clings so closely, and let us run with*
> *endurance the race that is set before us.*
> HEBREWS 12:1 ESV

PERSONAL APPLICATION:

Do you want to "begin again" in your walk with God? Is there something you've been "playing" at but now want to pursue "in earnest"? Maybe you want to grow in your daily devotions, join a Bible study, or find an accountability partner. Or perhaps you're ready to fully commit (or recommit) to following Jesus with all your heart.

God wants to do a new work in your life today! He is the God of new beginnings, revival, and renewal. Make it your prayer to "live a life worthy of the Lord and please him in every way: bearing fruit in every good work, growing in the knowledge of God" (Colossians 1:10 NIV). And if you've been trying to make this journey of faith on your own, join hands with your brothers and sisters in Christ. We all are pilgrims, and yet we are never alone.

PRAYER FOR TODAY:

Heavenly Father, I want to start fresh with You today. Please do a new work in me. I want to draw close to You and renew my commitment to follow You and love You all the days of my life. I give You my whole heart and soul. In those areas where I'm weary and need Your encouragement, please speak to my heart. I especially need Your strength to begin again in earnest in this area of my life: [your prayer]. In Jesus' name, amen.

"Love the Lord your God with all your heart and with all your soul and with all your strength and with all your mind."
LUKE 10:27 NIV

Day 2

THE LEAST
OF THESE

*"Truly I tell you, whatever you did for
one of the least of these brothers and
sisters of mine, you did for me."*
MATTHEW 25:40 NIV

Jo finds "a little crimson-covered book" under her pillow on Christmas morning—a copy of "that beautiful old story of the best life ever lived." It's described as a "true guidebook for any pilgrim going on a long journey."[1] Meg's copy is green, Beth's is dove, and Amy's is blue, each with "the same picture inside, and a few words written by their mother." Meg suggests that they "read a little every morning," a habit they've "neglected" since their lives were "unsettled" when Father went away. And they all settle down to read quietly for a half hour.

At breakfast their faith is quickly put to the test. As they prepare to eat the beautiful breakfast Hannah cooked and give their gifts to Marmee, Mrs. March comes in from visiting a "poor woman with a little newborn baby" and six hungry children "huddled into one bed to keep from freezing." She asks if they will give the Hummel family their breakfast as a Christmas present,

---

1 Amy's book is later referred to as a "testament" (ch. 19); thus, it's likely that these "guidebooks" are personal copies of *The New Testament*, though some readers believe they are copies of *Pilgrim's Progress* by John Bunyan.

and after a short pause, the four sisters quickly pack up their delicious feast.

At the Hummel home, they see things they've never encountered: "A poor, bare, miserable room. . .with broken windows, no fire, ragged bedclothes, a sick mother, wailing baby, and a group of pale, hungry children cuddled under one old quilt." They set to work quickly, building up the fire, caring for the mother, and feeding the children. Afterward Meg says, "That's loving our neighbor better than ourselves, and I like it."

The March sisters give away their breakfast and content "themselves with bread and milk," leaving "comfort behind" them. And the result is this: "there were not in all the city four merrier people." Haven't you found that to be true? When we give away our best, we come away with merry hearts! It's easier to give away our milk and bread instead of our "cakes and cream and. . .muffings" [sic], but it's a true sacrifice of praise to give away what we cherish most.

When you love and care for others, you show kindness to Jesus Himself. Jesus said, "I was hungry and you gave me something to eat, I was thirsty and you gave me something to drink, I was a stranger and you invited me in, I needed clothes and you clothed me, I was sick and you looked after me, I was in prison and you came to visit me" (Matthew 25:35–36 NIV). If you're wondering how you can possibly do any of those things for Jesus, Jesus explained it like this: "Truly I tell you, whatever you did for one of the least of these brothers and sisters of mine, you did for me" (Matthew 25:40 NIV).

And do not forget to do good and to share with others, for with such sacrifices God is pleased.
HEBREWS 13:16 NIV

PERSONAL APPLICATION:

Where can you "leave comfort behind" you in your daily life? What can you do in your home, in your neighborhood, or at your office or school to bring comfort to others? Ask God to show you how you can use your gifts to bless and love your neighbor as yourself today (Mark 12:31).

The March girls start their day with morning devotions, something they've neglected since "father went away" and the war "unsettled them". If they hadn't spent that first half hour of the day preparing their hearts, they might not have so cheerfully given their breakfast away. Do you have a time and a tucked-away place for your personal devotions? If not, think of ways to make that time special and make it a priority.

PRAYER FOR TODAY:

Thank You, Lord, for this reminder to prepare my heart through Bible reading and prayer each day. Please help me look for ways to love my neighbor, bless my family and friends, and leave comfort behind me wherever I go this week. When I am too focused on my own comfort, help me see other people's needs. Show me how I can bless these people today: [specific names]. In Jesus' name, amen.

A generous person will prosper; whoever refreshes others will be refreshed.
PROVERBS 11:25 NIV